Why I Married a Murderer
And How I Survived the Divorce

Ryan,
Thanks for all your help (listening to my crazy rants)

Teresa Roberts

by
Teresa X. Roberts

My Bipolar Express
Copyright © 2015 by Teresa Roberts

This is a work of creative nonfiction. The events are portrayed to the best of Teresa Roberts' memory. While all the stories in this book are true, some names and identifying details have been changed to protect the privacy of the people involved.

Cover design by Victor Marcos.
Illustrations by Charles L. Stephenson.
Edited by Evan David Zerhusen.

Third Edition

ISBN: 978-0-9910882-0-1

Acknowledgments

First and foremost I would like to thank all the assholes that have blessed me with their bullshit. Without them, I would have never dreamed of writing this book, nor would I have so much material, much of which I didn't even mention. I most certainly wouldn't have been the kicked in, broken down, knocked around, and bleeding profusely from the heart person that I once was, and hope to never be again.

I *am* grateful for every 'friend' who turned their back on me when I needed them most, because for every friend who walked away, two or three new friends and sometimes even complete strangers would enter my life, shining light upon my darkest days. For this reason, I highly encourage everyone to talk to strangers; they may just be angels in disguise. Or they could be real angels, or they could be evil and out to hurt you, you just never know. I still say you should take the chance. There are still more good people than bad I think. Anyway, eh hum....

I would like to give special thanks and gratitude for the loving shoulders that dried so many of my tears either physically, figuratively, or spiritually. They include the following in pretty much the order they came into my life: Angella and Debbie who were my best girlfriends in middle school and early high school, Teresa who was with me during our transition into adulthood,

Greg who was the meanest boyfriend I ever had, but we also had the most fun and he is one of the only two people I can honestly say I love unconditionally, Tracy who has always been there to help whether I wanted her to or not, Dan and Cheryl who have been there through thick and thin, Tony who was my angel from another planet (I hope he is hooting it up on the soul plane), Lora who I shared the most awesome 'couch & wine time' with, Novi who was as good for my soul as warm tea on a cloudy day, Brian who leads by example and is one of the most admirable people I know, Thomas who is an awesome attorney but an even better soul with gifts-a-plenty for his community, Pat and John who are like parents to me, only I really like them, both Dereks, one being a wonderful mother-hen when I needed it and the other the perfect verbal (and physical) wrestling partner, Scott whose calm nature helped me through stormy weather, Heather whose bizarre sense of humor was always a pleasant distraction from my brief ordinary moments, the Life Skills NW Class which was the perfect outlet at the perfect time, Eric my therapist who was simply the best, Shandi whose voice puts angels to shame, and last but not least, William and Kathy who own Zero Point and who have two of the purest hearts I have ever met.

I must also thank my sister Tena for being my sidekick growing up, my friend when I needed an ear, and for taking care of our Mother so well in her final years.

In wrapping the book up in preparation of getting it in your hot little hands, I would like to give credit where credit is due. Wait; maybe I was the one with the credit since I was always extending it to pay these guys! No seriously, I am not easily impressed, but I was blown away by how simple and user-friendly 99designs was to work with for cover art. My designer, Victor Marcos based in Manila, Philippines, is one bad-ass 99designer.

He was wonderful to work with and really put the icing on the cake. Note: This book is not a cake, you can *have* it, but you shouldn't eat it too. Bad idea.

Amazingly enough, I was equally, if not more so, impressed with the editor I found on Elance.com. Evan David Zerhusen won me over with his prompt turn-around times, excellent questioning to spark my memories and thoughts, and with wit quicker than Quick Draw Mcdraw. If you chuckle or laugh while reading my book, it is probably me, but if you pee your pants or snorked wine (or preferred beverage) out your nose, my editor may have helped with that, so thank him for the mess you just might make. Happy snorking!

I would also like to give a shout out to Terry O'Connor (www.inteleqt.com) who was my super hero web helper-outer, and to Ammy Anderson who *will* make a badass Burse out of this book (www.rockanovel.com).

Finally, I would like to give special thanks to Charles L. Stephenson who not only provided the awesome artwork throughout this book, but also for being a wonderful friend, who pushed, pulled, and supported me at the perfect times.

Charles lost his mother to cancer shortly before we started working together and I lost my mother to cancer just as I was finishing this book. To refer to our mothers as bookends may seem an odd compliment, however I feel it is appropriate. Mothers have a way of standing their ground and supporting just enough but not too much. They also hold knowledge, lessons learned, and stories that are nothing short of top shelf, stand the test of time, and are absolutely priceless. Therefore, in memory of our mothers, Sophie and Cherie, thank you for bringing Charles and me into this world so we could grow, learn, love, and connect with all the other souls who have made us who we are.

Author's Note
(Er, um, I mean Disclaimer)

In most cases, I have changed the names of the people who played a role in my life for both their protection and mine. If any name happens to be the same as your husband's, I promise... it wasn't him. I also may have compressed events by leaving out details that I did not feel pertained to *my* view of how events developed and unfolded (i.e., how shit went down). In some cases, I may also have included more details than necessary because, well, I'm a detailed kind of girl.

Conversations, correspondences, and events are rendered accurately to the best of my memory. Anger, frustration, bitterness, resentment, and a tad of jealousy may have made some events resonate more thoughts and feelings in me than in others that were in my life at various times. There was also no shortage of totally psychotic mind games that a few people played with my head that drove me to crazy town more times than I cared to visit. Yes, Yes, I know... *I* got in the car, but as you probably know from experience yourself, once it's going super-fast, up and down hills, around sharp corners and along steep edges, it's hard to just jump out.

A note about semi-colons; I like them; I don't know why. There are a lot of them in this book and most of them are improperly used; or so I'm told by an editor who I hired who quit after reading the first chapter (I think she had a semicolon phobia; she should probably not be an editor then; ya think?). The editor who stuck with me on the other hand is a dash man. At first I thought maybe he should join a 'Dash Support Group' or something but then I started getting used to them and realized, hey, dashes need love too, right?

Last, but certainly not least, thank *you* for purchasing this book. I would be honored if you also picked up one for a friend also. You can feel very confident that this book makes an excellent gift for anyone who also married a murderer. Just kidding; let's hope you don't have too many friends who did that; but I will bet you have a friend or two that survived a divorce, so pick up a copy for them and when they ask you what the hell you were thinking by buying them this book, just say "Oh, I just thought you liked semi-colons and dashes, and this book has *tons* of them."

Okay, this is really the last note: I also over use italics, quotes, uppercase, bold and underlines to show expression. If someone gave you this book to be considered for a proper punctuation and grammar award, it was clearly meant as a joke.

Preface
(We all know who's really to blame:
My Mom and Dad, of course.)

I'm not nuts. At least I've never had a doctor or medical professional say I was crazy, despite a few (former) friends, foes, and even a family member or two who most certainly thought I was/am.

"Why on Earth would a smart girl like you marry someone in prison, much less a *murderer*?" I heard more than a few times, to which I would smile and give varying answers depending on my mood or who asked the question.

Even though my upbringing could have been better (as I'm sure anyone can say), I still think that all kids should grow up, at least for the most part, like I did. I had a real mom and a real dad. I had real sisters and a real brother. I lived on a real farm in the Midwest. I played outside all day. I got dirty, I got hurt, I learned how to think and make quick decisions. Of course, I made some bad decisions, but everyone does. I got the belt—a *lot*. I got my hair pulled—a *lot*. But it was *real*—which is more than I can say for most of the people I see today. I learned the value (and sometimes the repercussions) of helping your neighbor whether you liked them or not. I learned to be independent. (When you live in the sticks, you figured out how to be self-sufficient and creative just as naturally as you figured out how to—well, you know.) I learned to be tough—to either sleep in the bed you made, or set it on fire with a vengeance and move on with your head held high ready to pay the piper, no matter the price.

I also learned to fall in love. No thanks to Mom and Dad (who I remember seeing kiss once, a peck, the entire time I grew up). Although I never saw them be affectionate, I figured out soon enough that they must have been intimate at least four times. They fought with passion; as in the kind you think of when you hear 'crime of passion'. It was totally normal to see my Dad staring out the window like a daydreaming zombie and then transition into verbal lashings seemingly out of nowhere in the matter of a split second. These outbursts were often followed by him biting his tongue while making a noise that sounded like he was revving up for some madman-rocket blast off. This eruption always included wildly swinging clenched fists, and more often than not, something getting broken. "We didn't *need* that [insert *something* we *really* needed] anyway," my Mom would usually say with a sarcastic tone after my Dad walked out of the house to cool off.

Of course my parents loved me; they just showed it in other ways. After all, they kept food on the table, clothes on my back, and a roof over my head. But I've since discovered that parents can do all of these things without really feeling the teeniest tiniest bit of love or affection for the people they do it for. It's like "duty" takes over—and from that point on, some parents run on auto-pilot, pulling the levers and the cranks, pushing the buttons and keeping the family machine going—duty-bound, honor-bound, whatever-bound—but love-bound? Not so sure. I really had occasion to wonder!

Let me start with Mom, after all, you'd think that's the first place you would find love, right? She once made me a snowmobile suit. Growing up in Minnesota, a snowmobile suit is as important of a piece of attire in the winter as sunglasses are in an Arizona summer. I was *thrilled* that my Mother made me a snowmobile suit because that meant I could stay outside and play longer in the cold. Even though I was only eight or nine at the time, however, I was smart enough to see her intentions were not all from the 'goodness of her heart'. She made it completely out of brown material – smack in the middle of deer hunting season. Every time I went outside to play I felt like I was being watched closely through high powered scopes. Um, now that I think about it, maybe she just wanted to make sure *someone* watched me. Yeah, sure, that's it!

One other time I suspected my Mother didn't love me was when I broke my leg trying to jump down an entire flight of steps. Showing off, of course! I slipped on the last step. My teacher and my Mother only ever knew of the last part of that statement. After hopping back up the three flights of stairs *alone* (all my friends wanted to play instead—and who can blame them?—it was recess time). I waited for the teacher to come back into the classroom. She was probably trying to take a break from us unruly kids. She called the principal, who also happened to be the father of a boy I had a slight crush on, and he helped me down the steps when Mom arrived to get me. I was apparently taking too long so he finally picked me up and carried me. My Mother just waited by the car. She had had to leave work—a thing she *never* did—and her eyes let me know she was not happy about it.

She drove me to the doctor which was just two blocks from the school in our small town. In her notable silence during the short drive she was probably thinking I could have hopped there instead of her taking time off work. At the doctor's office, she waited in the lobby while the nurse helped me hop to the examination room. It was the first time that I could recall ever being in one. It was cold and entirely too bright. I was *alone* when the doctor told me I had broken my leg, I was *alone* while he built the plaster cast around my foot and calf, and I was *alone* for what seemed like forever while I waited for it to dry.

On the way home, I told my Mom that the doctor said it would take twenty four hours to dry before I could walk on the rubber thing on the bottom, so I asked if I could get crutches. She snapped a cold, hard response "They cost too much." I asked if it was possible to rent them instead then, to which she then barked "No!" She *helped* me hop from the car to the house by holding my arm with a death grip for balance and got me to the couch. She then left me there and drove the nine miles back to work to finish her shift. I couldn't walk, and I was *alone*. I crawled down the long hall to the bathroom because I was afraid of falling while I was *alone*. I then crawled to the refrigerator in the kitchen and brought a bunch of snacks back to the couch.

It was during this time that I started to get a little pudgy. I always thought it was due to lack of activity, but I would later learn the term 'comfort food'. A therapist once told me that my Mom was only upset because she was worried about providing for the family—showing love in the only way she knew how, or something like that. I don't know. A little TLC may not seem like a big deal to adults—but it is to little kids—and it's not even something they need very much of. Just a look, a smile, a pat on the knee—anything to show that you give a damn—that's usually enough. And when a kid needs it, a kid needs it—more than air, or food, or anything else—even when it's the kid's own damn fault for getting hurt in the first place. Okay, okay, so we all blame our parents! But we know it's not *all* their fault, only partly.

So yeah, I admit, my therapist had a point—but I still thought it was pretty fucked up at the time.

*Disclaimer: My Mom actually did crochet some sort of cup looking thing to cover my toes when I had the cast on. I remember it had a thick elastic band to strap it around the back of my heel to stay on; and it was brown.

I knew my Dad loved me though. He would always tell me so as he was handing me a five dollar bill—and he wouldn't let it go until I said "I love you too". I suppose he was trying to teach me the value of politeness but it may have created one of my personality flaws as a side effect. I imagine this is where I learned that giving people things is how you show love. To this day, I can't break that habit. I am always buying things for people; even when I hate them (part of the 'kill them with kindness' theory). It's almost like an addiction. I'm pretty sure there are no rehab programs for compulsive givers, but I would definitely qualify for treatment if there were.

"Even assholes need love," a very old and dear friend once told me this after I shared the pain I went through during my divorce. I hadn't seen her in a very long time, as we both had moved away from each other. She had found God sometime back so when she said that during our parting embrace, it meant more to me than it probably would have from anyone else. I'm pretty sure Jesus would have said it a little differently—but, what the hell; the message would've been the same, right?

One thing I have learned about love and relationships now that I'm older, is that people are not jerks *all* the time, nor did they most likely act like that in the beginning. I probably knew that when I was young too—but somewhere along the way we forget this basic stuff and dwell on our injuries and insults. My first divorce—believe it or not—was a breeze; almost too easy. The second divorce felt like he raked broken glass over my open and bleeding heart. Yet, I still have trouble accepting when people do nothing but bash their exes. It puzzles me that they don't see how it reflects on them; they picked their mate, were with them, married them, and sometimes had children with them after all. Either there must have been some redeeming quality at some point or they should admit that they are just really stupid for hooking up with a jerk. Let me just state for the record right here: I've made some bad decisions in *my* past (hense the book you are about to read) that were nothing short of stupid.

However, I *can* honestly say my first husband was a *wonderful* man. He was smart—like, genius smart. He was funny; he left me the sweetest sticky notes with hilarious drawings on them. He was caring and helped any friend in need at the drop of a hat. My second husband was also very smart, funny, and kind. He was a talented artist and he also had a way with words (good and bad). He also had the most beautiful eyes that made me melt. I don't regret falling in love or marrying either of them. I learned and grew a lot from both experiences, as well as from other non-marital relationships I've had.

I've learned there are many kinds of love. I think the most important thing I've learned is that, even though you think your world has come to an end, you simply must continue on and start again.

Contents

The World Wide Web of Dating Hell 1

First Crush 11

Bruiser 20

Anger Ball 29

No Safe Bets 40

Comfort Food is a Killer 59

Losing More than My Marriage 67

Life is Short – Play Naked 74

The Best Breaker-Upper 83

Love at First ~~Strike~~ Sight 96

The Power of the Written Word 106

Paper Proposal 115

First Kiss 118

First Fight 123

Not the Average Wedding Drama 131

Moving Closer to the Truth 141

Pardon Me 150

The Beginning of the End 158

A Chance for a Fresh Start 175

Hitting Bottom 186

Finding a Positive Path 195

I Am... Back 203

AddenDUM 212

The Psycho Sequel 217

The World Wide Web of Dating Hell

Online dating was invented by the devil. Or maybe it was invented by Al Gore, since I heard a rumor that he invented the Internet. No seriously, I think Satan himself created online dating purely for his sick and twisted sense of humor, but also to show the world how we really are deep down inside—lonely, horny, pathetic, desperate and/or completely full of shit.

It *seems* like the easy thing to do—just write a little blurb about who you are, what you're looking for, what you're *not* looking for, and voilà, the exact person of your dreams will appear in your inbox in mere moments.

But instead, if you're a 35-45 year old woman you get ten emails from dirty old men wanting a younger

1

woman, eight emails from college boys wanting a cougar, four emails containing pictures of the sender's penis with the entire content of the email saying: "hit me up if you're interested," and at least one email bashing you for something you asked for that the responder is *not*, telling you how shallow, superficial, and/or racist you are, in addition to some colorful names. I am going to go out on a limb here and guess that this last person is the one who flagged your ad for deletion so you will *never* find true love. Why? Because they can cowardly hide behind the electronic curtain of anonymity, where all is safe, while they are in their Mother's basements.

However, if you're a man, of any age, you're really in luck. You get 142 emails from women of your dreams; they are all new to online dating, they've *never* done this before, and they are ready to do anything your heart desires—right after you click a link, enter your credit card, and kiss your money and/or identity goodbye. Why? Because they can hide where all is safe, in a luxury condo bought and paid for by idiot men too scared to meet a real woman, who live, where all is safe, in their Mother's basements.

I have actually been on countless dates originating from online connections. I once was chatting with a guy for a few days and when we finally met in person, he breathed like a Sleestak from *The Land of the Lost*. Don't get me wrong, I was a big fan of the show, but I just couldn't handle that breathing during our lunch date, let alone think about what he might sound like during sex. He may have even been having sex with himself *then*, under the table, now that I think about it; which might explain *why* he sounded like a Sleestak.

After chatting online with another guy for a while, we met up to see a movie. During the opening credits he started making out with me. When I jerked away to indicate I was not interested in making out during the movie like a couple of school kids, he pouted for the next two hours. He texted me a couple days later to apologize for his forwardness. I thought that was sweet and I was about to give him another chance. Just then he sent another text saying he would like to make it up to me by 'treating me' to oral sex for lunch. I truly wish I was making this up!

Then there was the guy who on our first (and only) date told a pubic hair joke *while* we were eating dinner, which involved a spitting gesture—*at* the table, *in* the restaurant. There was one guy who constantly played video poker at the bar while asking me odd questions, never making eye contact during the whole first date (there was no second date). There was a guy who insisted on meeting right away for a drink and then complained for 45 minutes about how tired he was from getting sunburned and drinking at NASCAR all day. Then there was a guy who was a taxi cab driver who told me story after story of the life of a cab driver; as sad as it was, I actually found our date to be refreshing after some of the previous ones.

Maybe I come off a little too snarky? Well—I can't help it. Okay, my therapist tells me I can but won't, so there you have it—the fact of the matter straight from a professional. The point is, 1) I've tried keeping comments to myself, but 2) it pisses me off when people say I don't give men a 'chance'. I give them chances all day long—in fact, my next book is going to be about exactly how many chances I've given them. The problem with men is—*they're men*.

Okay, so I said it. Don't take it the wrong way!

Back to my point. Online dating should come with a disclaimer: 'purely for entertainment purposes only'—like seeing a psychic or playing the lottery. That said, I must confess, I have met three amazing people from personal ads.

One was from an ad I placed in the newspaper before the Internet existed (that's how far back *I* go—so show some respect, huh?). I was just looking for friends, male or female, who among other things were fans of *The X-Files*. I asked responders to write to a P.O. Box. My thought was that if they were willing to make the effort to write a letter, put it in an envelope, put a stamp on it, and mail it, they might, just might, be a quality person who *also* really wanted a quality friend.

I got a letter from a girl who wrote a brief, but funny letter; it read: "I like *The X-Files* too, but just so you know, Fox Mulder will be *my* husband someday so you can't have him." Through the ups and downs over the years, she and I are still friends almost 20 years later (I can't believe how time flies).

The other two quality people I met online, *(amazingly enough)* were in Reno. I say *amazingly enough*, not only because I met them online, but also because, well, if you ever lived in Reno, you would understand. After living there a few years, I *get* why Johnny Cash wrote a song about shooting a man in Reno just to watch him die.

Eh hem… anyway; one of these gems, with whom I am still friends, met me at the Little Nugget for an Awful Awful Burger. (Note: If you ever go to Reno, you **must** have one; they are Awfully, Awfully Good!) He suggested we share a burger which I was totally down for since I've had the gastric bypass surgery (and they *give* you enough fries to feed all the panhandlers in front of the place until *they* are stuffed). So my new friend got some unexpected brownie points for offering to share a burger.

It is odd in itself for a man to not eat a 'manly' portion and actually *want* to share a meal, but the truly impressive part came almost two years later when I learned that not only was he a vegetarian, but also a total health nut who had competed in multiple Iron Man competitions. Wow, a vegetarian who didn't throw a fit about the meeting place, but suffered through red meat *and* greasy fries to have a date with me. Big gold star! Though no sparks flew over the mountain of fries we shared, we are *still* very good friends.

And last but not least, I met a cop from an online ad. My ad said that I was married, but in an open relationship and I just wanted someone to hang out with, go to movies with, etc. His response to my ad was "I am also married, but in an open relationship and would love to be friends, or more. However, I'm a cop; I hope that doesn't scare you." I responded right away with "I'm married to a murderer in prison; I hope *that* doesn't scare *you*."

We agreed to meet, but I insisted that at some point in the near future I also needed to meet his wife to make sure everything was 'cool'. He said, "You will meet her at the same time you and I meet; how about tonight?" We all got along great and have been friends ever since.

Sadly, my list of success stories with personal ads pretty much ends there. I once met a guy online who was about my age and who I thought was great at first. He was from upstate Wisconsin (I'm from Minnesota), had a great job, sounded old fashioned, sweet, etc. Later I learned he was suspended from his job, slept on an air mattress at a friend's house, was obsessed with making his (air) bed and judged people harshly who didn't make their beds first thing in the morning. I try to understand and have compassion for people who are going through transitions in their lives. Hell, most of the time my middle name is transition. I looked past all that, but texting me first thing in the morning asking what color panties I was wearing (we had only met once and had not even kissed) was where I finally drew the line and told him I wasn't really interested. That's when the real fun began.

My big mistake was trying to be nice about it. I tried to fix him up with a friend of mine and he ended up blowing her phone up with texts bashing me and then asked her to go on a 'road trip' to Hawaii. Ding, ding, ding, we have a winner! NOT.

There was another 'almost' success story. After several texts with a great sounding guy, we agreed to meet for lunch. I was really excited since this was the first guy, in a long while, who had managed to last a week or so without saying (or sending pictures of) anything sexual. A half hour before we were to meet for lunch, he texted me a picture of his penis. I texted back "Why did you do that?" He responded, "I just wanted to make sure you were still interested before I wasted my time." (Texted straight, where all is safe, from his Mother's basement, I am quite sure.)

I would be rich if I had a nickel for every time someone said to me "Find ways to meet people other than online; join a singles hiking club, get out more, or ask your friends to introduce you to someone they know."

This advice always makes me either laugh so hard that I pee my pants a little, makes me want to slap them, or pisses me off. It almost always sparks a challenge in the form of an argument, or an argument in the form of a challenge depending on the mood I am in at the time.

I usually start out by siding with these 'you-know-nothing-at-all-about-dating-these-days' people by saying something like, "Ya know, you're right! I don't know why I am looking online when my ideal man is a construction worker or some sort of skilled tradesman who wouldn't know how to turn a computer on if his life depended on it." Just when the person I am talking to smiles and says in their most cocky tone, "See, you're looking in the wrong place for what you want, that's why you never find it and are *always* disappointed." That's when I pull out my arsenal of verbal arrows and start loading my bow, flinging one sarcastically snide remark after another: "Right, I should start hanging out at construction sites or aimlessly walk up and down the aisles at Home Depot. Or maybe I should go hang out at construction bars on Fridays when they are cashing their paychecks, so I can land one who drinks, smokes, and pisses their money away before they go back to work on Monday. Oh, and I am so sure that I would find the construction type man I am looking for in a hiking club because most men who are on their feet all day building houses or laying concrete probably love going on hikes too. Or maybe I might meet one of those kinda guys at the library; I hear construction guys just love hanging out at the library."

I ask my construction type guy-friends all the time if they know any *good guys* that they work with. I get the same response every time followed by rolling laughter, "I wouldn't fix you up with *anyone* I know, they are all piece of shit assholes."

Teresa X. Roberts

I did have a friend of mine set me up once with his friend Adam. My friend knew both Adam and his wife and said they had been separated for almost a year. My friend had just gone to her house to do some repairs and had also been to his place to BS and have a couple beers, so it would seem safe to assume he was in fact single. My friend tells me that Adam really needed to get out and have some fun, so I invited him to a concert. It was pure hell! He spent the entire evening complaining about his soon-to-be ex-wife and how he is living in a hotel room while she has the house that he is still paying for and she is raping him for child support, blah, blah, blah. I couldn't wait for the date to end and almost peeled away before he was completely out of the car.

About a week later, I got a call at 1:30am from a woman screaming at me. "DID YOU HAVE FUN WITH MY HUSBAND ON YOUR DATE?" I didn't recognize the number so I wiped the sleep from my eyes and tried to calmly say, "Who is your husband?" I was really hoping this chick had the wrong number but she continued to scream at me "Oh, you're fucking so many married men you can't keep track of them all?" I was just lying there, sleeping, *alone* in my bed, like I did *every* night. I was still holding out hope that she had misdialed. I said again, in an even calmer voice, "Please tell me who your husband is." She responded venomously, "ADAM!"

I honestly don't know what I was thinking--oh, yeah, it was 1:30am, I *wasn't* thinking, and certainly wasn't thinking about the date I had a week ago that I forgot the moment it was over. So I said, "I know about five Adam's (which was true), can you be more specific?" That didn't help matters at all. I had to hold the phone away from my ear while I heard what a home-

8

wrecker I was to poor married (psycho) women all over town!

I let her scream at me for a minute or two before it dawned on me who her husband must be. When she took a breath, I explained that I was told they were separated for almost a year, to which she informed me that they just slept together last night (good for her, like I care, I thought). She continued to scream at me. By then I'd had enough and I finally yelled back, "What am I supposed to do, hook my dates up to lie detector tests? Why don't you yell at your jerk husband who is apparently lying and cheating? But just for the record, our 'date' sucked because all he did was complain about what a bitch you are, which I now believe to be the *one true thing* he *did* tell me," and I hung up.

I wish I could say that was the only angry wife phone call I ever received as a result of men saying they were single when in fact they were not. This is one reason why swing clubs not only exist, but also are thriving under-the-radar businesses these days—but that's another story for another time.

I'm not a big fan of baseball—or of sports in general. Okay, maybe motocross, but I like the smell and sound of it more than anything. Okay, maybe I like the idea of metaphorically 'grabbing the bull by the horns' so to speak, and having that kind of control to go forward in any direction I choose. But back to my lack of lust for baseball before I get carried away by catching air on the double jumps in my head; I think it's fair to say I was 'striking out' on the dating field.

So, the million dollar question is 'why would a smart girl like me marry someone in prison, a murderer no less?' Well...it all started back in *'Nam*. Just kidding, I just like saying that sometimes, with an old geezer dialect of course. Yes, I realize you want to know, but what kind of book would this be if I told you at the end of chapter one? Grab a beer, chai tea, or a brandy snifter (full of brandy, of course) and a calabash pipe (but only if you're wearing a plaid bathrobe and bunny slippers) and sit for a spell already; the dirty dishes aren't going anywhere.

First Crush

I grew up as a tomboy, as many farm girls do out of necessity to merely survive in their environment every day. I actually did try, once, to be friends with a neighbor girl who did *not* live on a farm. She was into dolls and such, and for some strange reason, I had a couple of dolls that she didn't have, so I worked that angle to be friends with her.

Mind you, I did not *want* to be friends with her at all, but I caved to pressure from my Mom that I should stop hanging around boys so much. Against my better judgment, I told the bus driver (who was also a neighbor and knew my parents) that it was okay with my Mom that I got off the bus with this girl at her house and that my Mom would be picking me up later; I was only eight or ten years old at the time. I honestly had no idea how I was really going to get home, which was not really that far by car, but way too far for a kid that age to walk.

We got off the bus together and walked up the long driveway to the singlewide trailer she lived in on a little chunk of land her family owned. As soon as we walked in the door, her aunt presented her with a gift; her very own Barbie doll (the exact one that I had, that she didn't). She squealed with excitement and promptly told me I could go home now. Wow – that was harsh!

That moment alone convinced me that boys were way better friends than girls were. The boys I hung out with were cool, not judgmental, not snotty, and most important, they didn't squeal with joy when they got a new toy. Instead, they quickly gathered their friends to share it with.

Because I hung out with boys, and we got to be such close friends, there was occasional 'practicing' on one another as we entered our teens. It was all pretty harmless with the utmost respect and politeness, and it was always for 'educational' purposes only, of course. For some reason, we had the maturity to understand that just because we practiced French kissing on each other, and maybe a few other things, we knew that it didn't mean we were going steady or anything. I will never forget the first time my friend Ben put his tongue in my mouth. I spit it out like it was the most disgusting thing ever. It's a funny thing though; I remember that kiss like it was yesterday, but don't have a clue who, what, when, or where my first real 'romantic' kiss took place. Obviously, there were no fireworks.

Even though my friends and I would 'mess around' as we called it then, I never felt cheap or like I was a slut or anything. We kept pretty busy doing extremely productive kid stuff—like building forts out of lumber that our parents probably *needed* for something important, digging through rotten hay looking for grubs to use as fishing bait, climbing fire watch towers that were chained off and 'forbidden', and walking on barely frozen over creeks, alone, and way too far from "help me, I'm drowning and freezing to death" yelling distances. With all the things we felt we needed to conquer as learning and growing kids, there really wasn't much time for 'messing around'.

I did have one girl friend, Carrie, who lived several miles from me. I remember how confused I was when Carrie's parents would never allow her to spend the night at my house because 'I hang around boys.' I even seem to recall there was a reference from her parents that I was 'loose.' I was very puzzled, because I was most definitely not 'boy crazy' like her parents thought I was. Other than the fact that I went in the house to pee instead of behind a tree in the yard, I *was* a boy as far as I was concerned. I would have much rather been a tomboy than a squealing, snotty girl any day, after all. The funny thing about Carrie was that she ended up getting knocked up by her cousin at the young age of fifteen, *after* I moved away out of state.

Despite the fact that I was a tomboy, that didn't change 'nature' from happening. My very first crush, Doug, was a few years older than I was and he was just as rebellious as he was cute. He was one of seven kids in a hardworking Minnesota family of farmers. I, like many others in a small Midwest community, were taught from a young age that working hard should be your *only* priority and goal in life. Owning your own farm, even if it's just a house with a barn used only to store junk in, is the only dream you need to worry your little head about. Goals and dreams tend to not extend much beyond the pastures or the next harvesting season in a Midwest farming community.

Doug, like many kids of farming families, saw little need for schooling much after the 7th grade since there was always more important work to be done at home. At about 15 years old, Doug landed a coveted job at the largest restaurant in town (there were only three total). I think he started out as a bus boy but was quickly promoted to cook, which simultaneously promoted the size of his ego around our little town. Of course, because he could pull it off, his cocky attitude made him all the more alluring to a young girl who had just started noticing boys.

I think he actually quit school about ten minutes after I realized I had a crush on him. He figured he didn't have time to help on the farm, go to work, *and* school. Something had to give and school was the logical choice to a farmer. Since it was pretty instilled in me from a young age that having a job (or working on a farm) was the only dream or goal to have, Doug became pretty attractive to me because he figured that out so early; that, and did I mention, he was insanely cute?

There was a church down the road, which was always unlocked for the good people in our community who were always welcome to go in and pray. I, however, being the mischievous young teen that I was, would go into the church office and use the phone to call Doug. In a small town, everyone knows what you've done before you even think about doing it. The church sharing a phone line with one of the nosey neighbors helped speed up this process in my case. Looking back, it's amazing the amount of stupid shit I tried to pull know-

ing that we were a party-line phone call away from being ratted out. It was embarrassing then, but of course,
pretty funny now.

***

My Dad worked up north in the iron ore mines. He
stayed up there during the week and slept in the car in
front of his brother's house. My Uncle wouldn't let him
in because he was so dirty. When us kids were young,
Dad would come home and give all the change in his
pocket to whoever rushed to take his dirty boots off for
him. I remember this chore fondly. As we got older,
we began to dread Friday nights, as they were then for
our spank'ns that we earned all week while he was
gone. We quickly learned that we had Monday and
Tuesday to be bad, but we had better redeem ourselves
by the time Dad called on Wednesday night to check up
on us.

My Mom pulled off sometimes as many as three jobs
at one time, as well as keeping the pigs and us kids fed.
Despite both parents working, we always seemed to be
poor. Dressing like a penniless farmer in clothes that
were either handed down from who knows where,
mended with patches, or—God forbid—that Mom made
us, ensured that I didn't exactly fit with the 'in' crowd at
school. It didn't matter that the 'in' crowd in a town of
1,200 was pretty small, and not really that 'in' anyway.

At 13 years old I got a job bussing tables where my
Mom worked as a cook. I often got off the bus there after school and hung out until she got off work anyway. I
earned $1.50/hr plus a share of the tips, all under the
table. They called me 'the kid' which was short for 'So-

phie's kid'. Now that I was making my own money, the first thing I did was became human, as far as I was concerned. I started buying my own clothes, got my ears pierced, and permed my hair; my first taste of being an individual.

***

I am the oldest of three girls and one boy so I didn't have older siblings to 'show me the way'. My Mom was way too busy to teach me how to fix my hair cute, and she probably had no clue how to work a curling iron anyway, or even time to talk to me about my period. Oh, my period, now that's a funny story!

As I said before, we were poor, so birthday gifts could never be counted on or barely even hoped for. However, we could always count on Aunt Ellen to send a card on our birthdays with a five dollar bill in it. So, one day when I was about 10, my Mom handed me a box and said, "You got something in the mail. Go to your room and open it." Puzzled, because it was not near my birthday or Christmas, I had no clue what it could have been. I started opening it right there in the dining room. My Mom quickly snapped at me, "GO TO YOUR ROOM to open it!" Okay, Okay, fine, so I went to my room to open it, geez.

It was a booklet about what to expect when you get your period, along with some 'sample' products. I have to say, the giant not-so-luxury yacht looking pad with a strap contraption thing scared me half to death.

My Mom wouldn't talk to me about my period at all, but of course as soon as I got it about a year later; she announced it to all her friends, in front of me, as if she was proud. My jaw dropped open in awe, followed by a dramatic eye roll, followed by a swift exit.

Once I started dressing and looking like a girl, the other girls actually started to treat me like one. It was an odd feeling—as if I'd switched teams or something. My boy-friends were also starting to grow beyond back yard football games and bike rides to the park. They were starting to think about putting their earlier 'practicing' to more productive and rewarding efforts, so I thought it was time I did too.

Somehow, I got the attention of a new boy who just moved to town named Franky. We started liking each other and he bought me a bracelet with his name on it. I thought it was sweet, but weird. The only thing a boy had given me before that, was his ABC gum, which he made seem like it should have been an honor for me to receive. Franky came with me to my job one day and everyone there ooh'd and ahh'd about him; "He's so cute." "He looks like a nice boy." "Oh kid, you're growing up." They all chanted one by one. I broke up with him shortly thereafter as I lost interest and didn't care for the girly attention I was getting. I just wanted to work and play.

***

My Dad got a job in Nevada and us kids were told we would be selling just about everything we own to move there. I was 14 or 15 at the time. As I understood it, Doug's parents (Doug, my first crush) owed us some money for allowing them the use of our land to grow crops, so my parents struck a deal with them to help us get out to Nevada as part of the repayment.

I am not sure why, but we all spent the night at Doug's family's house the night before we took off even though they lived just a few miles from us. That night, I snuck into Doug's room hoping to *talk* one last time before I left. *He* wanted to feel my boobs and he couldn't understand why I wouldn't let him. When I denied his advances, he said, "What did you sneak in my room for then?" This would be the first time, but certainly not the last, I thought, 'Boys are so dumb and they just don't get it'. I felt like only my boobs mattered; not me. Sometimes I *still* feel this way.

We had all our worldly possessions in the back of their long bed two-toned green Ford pick-up truck, and Mom and us kids were in our baby blue K-Car Station Wagon as we headed off the next morning to our new unknown life in the Nevada desert. Considering we had a family of six, I can't believe how we got down to having all of our worldly (okay, Minnesotan) possessions in the back of one pickup truck. Thinking back to what we *did* bring, I can't imagine we had more than one change of underwear to our names.

Doug's parents had probably never been more than 80 miles away from their farm at that point of their lives so I suppose this was quite an adventure for them too. It was also probably the first time they had to trust their kids to take care of the farm for more than one feeding or milking. That had to be pretty stressful for them— and pretty neat, yet scary for their kids.

The hot and dry desert of Nevada is about as far removed from the humid, lake-filled, tree-covered lands of Minnesota as a person could get, so it took a while to adjust.

Two memories stand out other than getting used to the new geography. I had never heard of the Mormon religion before, so the first time I heard a kid refer to someone as a Mormon, I thought it was a derogatory insult because it sounded like moron.

The other new vocabulary word for me was *burrito*. The first time I heard a kid say he ate a couple burritos for lunch, I thought he meant an animal like a Burro, so I was both horrified, yet impressed, when he said he ate not one, but two of them. We had tacos in our small town, but at that time, there wasn't much in the way of ethnic culture or diversity. I don't recall any Mexican kids in our school ever, and I remember when the one and only black kid came to our high school. Boy did I feel sorry for him. I don't remember anyone being mean or anything. People were still too busy judging the local Indians (as in Native Americans). It was only the beginning of learning new things.

Bruiser

We spent only six months in Indian Springs, Nevada, before moving to the big town of Pahrump on the other side of the mountain range. Just when I thought I was getting used to the geographical, ethnic, religious, and outdoor recreational differences, I found I could still be surprised by learning even more. I learned that just because it's called a Chicken Ranch, Mustang Ranch, or Bunny Ranch, that doesn't mean it has anything to do with 'farm animals', then again, for enough money, it just might.

***

Some friends of my parents had come out from Minnesota looking for work just before we moved from Indian Springs to Pahrump. I would imagine finances played a part in the genius decision by the adults that we would all live in a tiny two-bedroom trailer. When I say 'we all', I mean two sets of parents and six kids. My Mom called it the 'tuna can', and for good reason. It was maybe nine feet wide by maybe 30 feet long and the second bedroom had enough room for me to lean against the bunk bed while sitting on the floor and stretching out my legs to touch the wall. I only recall sharing that room with my younger brother so looking back, I can't imagine how uncomfortable everyone *else* had to be stacked together, which makes me wonder why Mom didn't call it the 'sardine can'.

This *cozy* predicament promptly ended when my brother got in trouble with the boy in the other family for breaking into a little craft store down the road and stealing some model car kits. My parents were furious that they tried to help these people, took them in, fed them, and *their* kid got my brother in trouble. Of course, it was embarrassing for them too, but I am pretty sure my brother's arm wasn't the one being twisted.

Even after they moved out, the tension in the tuna can was still as high as the desert summer was hot. As the other family was settling in next door, in a smaller trailer just 15 feet away, my Mom noticed them unpacking boxes and boxes of food they had stored in their truck. I remember her screaming, waiving her arms in the air in our tiny living room as she peered out the lace curtains at them, "Where was this food when they stayed *here*?" I'm pretty sure what she *really* meant was, "Well, those ungrateful Mother Fuckers!"

We played outside as much as humanly possible which was quite a challenge being we didn't have grass for football, creeks for swimming or fishing, or trees to build forts in. What the hell are you supposed to do to play on dirt that is hard as concrete? There is a plant in the desert commonly known as a Goat Head. This seemingly friendly *looking* plant has thorns, that amazingly enough look like a Goat's Head with three points that are razor sharp. After stepping on my first Goat Head, not only did I *not* want to play outside again, but I wanted to set fire to every evil desert plant I saw.

The first day I went to school in this new little town, we played a game in PE called 4-square. I couldn't wrap my mind around how completely sissy this game was and how totally unphysical it was. In Minnesota, we played flag football and baseball in the summer, archery in the fall, and broom hockey, dodge ball, and snowshoe walks in the winter.

The only thing we ever did one year in Phy-Ed (as we called it back home) that wasn't extremely physical, was learned sign language. We had a deaf kid at our school for a while, so to communicate with him, we used our Phy-Ed time to learn sign language. The deaf kid used to pull girls' hair, especially those who had really long hair because he *could* hear them when they screamed. We figured out pretty quickly this was the same reason he often pulled the school fire alarm.

It was annoying of course, but it *was* kinda funny to watch him be giddy with excitement when he could hear, for just that moment. We got used to taking our lunch trays out with us when the alarm went off, and the girls with long hair were told to just scream at him when they saw him coming so he wouldn't 'have to' pull their hair. It wasn't until then that I stopped hating the pixy cut my Mom kept my hair in.

So anyway, the second day of school in Pahrump, when I overheard some girls saying they were thinking about playing football with the boys in P.E., I chirped up "we can do that?—Play with the boys?" It was truly a joyous moment for me. We all walked out to the sparsely covered grass field that sprinklers desperately tried to keep green. We were given no flag attire so my logical assumption was that we were playing tackle.

On the first play, I took my classmate, Gary down with all the grace of a bulldozer hopped up on Mt. Dew and Pop Rocks. Although it was a completely familiar behavior for me, to my surprise everyone seemed really impressed and started saying I was an animal. That fed my ego just a tad, so on the second play, I repeated my 'just another day of playing with the boys' behavior. Shortly after, as my team started spewing kudos and compliments, the P.E. teacher marched over with saliva flying out of his mouth as he was yelling at me. "We don't have equipment to play like that—settle down." Huh? What on earth was he talking about, I thought. Turns out, it was 'two hand touch' football, which of course, I had never heard of in my life.

Hector, another classmate, later wrote an 'official document' declaring my new nickname of Bruiser along with all the gory details, though extremely exaggerated, as to how I earned it. I would be known as Bruiser from that day forward. Even teachers often called out Bruiser during roll calls. Part of the reason it stuck with teachers could have had something to do with the fact that there was almost always another Teresa, and my last name being polish. Philipczyk looks hard to say, but we've always pronounced it *Flip-sick*. When explaining to people how to say it, I always said 'like you *flipped* over and got *sick*; Flip-Sick.' However, teachers would always struggle with it when they saw it so 'Bruiser' became my roll-call name so they didn't look stupid trying to say my real last name.

When I was 15, I met Ivan who lived down the road from us and who was a few years older than me. He was a senior and I was a freshman. Ivan treated me like a real girl and snapped at everyone who called me Bruiser. That name might as well have been on my birth certificate as far as most of the town was concerned so he eventually gave up fighting that battle. We dated for one year and three months, which is a long time when you're that young. Ivan had a job as a dishwasher and was a hard worker, which was attractive to me. He also treated me very well. He bought me a cubic zirconium ring from the Sears catalog and we were going to get married! Uh-huh (as I do an eye roll now)!

My parents were too busy trying to keep my brother out of trouble and food on the table to notice much of what I was doing at the time. They were pretty indifferent to Ivan for the most part. Thinking back, I don't think I really loved Ivan all that much. I was young, of course, and didn't know what the word meant in relation to a, well, relationship. We got along, we were intimate, and we were dating exclusively. I guessed that's what love meant at the time.

I was almost 16 when I got sick with the flu and asked my Dad to take me to the doctor. We had one doctor in town that was rumored as a quack but what do you do when he's the only one? My Dad gave me $25 and told me to have Ivan take me. I was explaining to the doctor that I have the flu, and suddenly without any warning or preparation at all, he lifted up my shirt and looked at my boobs. After a brief gander at my nipples, he announced, "You're pregnant."

"Uh... no...I have the flu!" I said. He completely dismissed *my* diagnosis and said, "Do you want me to make *sure* you're pregnant?" I don't even remember answering him but I *do* remember him sticking cold salad tong looking tools up my hoo-haw. "Yep, your about six weeks along, it looks good. Do you know what you're going to do?" He said while talking into my vagina. I stared blankly at the old stained panels in the ceiling trying to wrap my head around how having the flu made me pregnant. "Well, you can't have an abortion or you'll go to hell," he muttered as he walked out the door leaving me in my deer-in-the-headlights daze with the nurse to finish the conversation (or lecture).

At least I *think* there was a conversation or lecture. I was 15 years old and all I can *remember* thinking is that I had the flu—and somehow that made me pregnant. It felt like the worst word problem in math I had ever had to figure out: *So, two trains without brains, who thought they could climb any mountain as long as they had enough money for fuel and a burger and fries, somehow derailed because a gnat hit the conductor in the eye ball. If the gnat was black and the conductor was white...Wait..................* HOW THE FUCK DOES HAVING THE FLU MAKE ME PREGNANT?

My mind was going a million miles an hour with the emergency brake on. Of course, Ivan and I talked about it a bit, but for the most part I think he was just as shocked as I was. We were both feeling pretty numb (and dumb, I suppose). Needless to say, we didn't come to any decision right away. Later that night, at a school basketball game, Ivan's brother came up to me and quietly said, "If you need anything or need to talk, let me know." Okay, that was odd. I found Ivan and asked him if he had told him. He replied, "No, he happened to go to the doctor today after we left and the nurse opened your medical chart, pointed to where it said 'six weeks pregnant' and said "maybe you should talk to your little brother about this." Ya just gotta love small towns!

Ivan had heard from a very close source that one of the cheerleaders had gotten an abortion. I knew I couldn't go to my parents for information about the topic since I wasn't even allowed to ask questions about my period. One, I wasn't ready to tell either of them, and two, they probably wouldn't have been willing to interrupt their lives or expend any time or money for a medical condition I got myself into anyway.

I nervously penned a note to the cheerleader that was not only much older than me, but one of the most popular girls in the school. It was safe to say I was *not* in her circle by any meaning of the word. I wrote that I knew I was risking a lot by telling her this, but that I was pregnant and that I heard she had an abortion. I told her I would never tell anyone, whether or not she helped me, but I would really appreciate any advice she was willing to share. I got a hall pass so no one would see me put the note in her locker, and anxiously waited. Would she help me or would she show the note to all her friends and make me the laughing stock of the school? The latter seemed much more likely.

The very next break between classes she handed me a note, in plain sight of *everyone*. I was shocked, excited, sweating, panicking, and speechless. The next few moments until I could get into my next class to read it seemed to last forever. I was shaking uncontrollably when I unfolded the notebook paper and began to read what would surely change my life forever. She wrote the name of her doctor, told me how much it cost, told me what to expect, and wrote that if I had any questions or needed any help, to just ask. Her willingness to share knowledge with me despite the risk that I could have ruined her reputation was a pivotal point in my life.

Ivan and his Mother took me to get an abortion on my 16th birthday.

A few months later, Ivan started taking an interest in a new girl, and we somehow broke up despite him never bothering to mention it to me. I pretty much figured it out when he left to go into the military, and didn't stop by to say good-bye. It became *very* clear when his friend asked for all his things back. Everyone said I should have kept the beautiful cubic zirconium ring from Sears, but I returned it along with a garbage bag full of other stuff including his letterman's jacket and a pillow his Grandmother had embroidered for him.

***

I mostly hung out with the stoner crowd after Ivan and I parted, mainly because they had the most parties. The jocks would occasionally throw one when their parents were out of town, but theirs were always stuffy and had odd rules about them, like not getting drunk and breaking things, or puking on the furniture. The stoner crowd, on the other hand, didn't need any stink'n house; any random road out in the middle of the desert did just fine. In fact, those parties were more fun because there was usually a fire to gather around, nothing much to break or hurt ourselves on, everyone kept their beer in coolers in their own cars, and you could puke just about anywhere. (I am quite sure no one *ever* drove drunk though).

Anger Ball

I always enjoyed people watching more than 'participating' (or I should say 'indulging') at parties. One person I got a kick out of observing was Jack. Jack would wear these crazy looking Army pants that had pockets everywhere. They were similar to parachute pants, which were popular at that time, but these were made of a khaki material and were very lose fitting. When we were at the same parties, I noticed throughout the night that his pants seemed to get thicker as the hours passed. He would also walk slower as the night drew on, which could easily be attributed to continue drinking, but something told me there was more to it.

I finally approached Jack and inquired about his *interesting* pants. He tried to be sly and attempted to convince me that it is my imagination (or drinking) that made me think there is something peculiar about them, but he eventually let me in on his little secret. He would wonder around bumming beers off of people all night and stuffing them in the numerous pockets.

He later shared his very elaborate strategies, including who he would approach first, last, and how often in between; he had quite a system. Of course, since none of us should have been drinking in the first place, he sometimes justified his way of acquiring alcohol by saying that he was just ensuring that *they* didn't drink too much before driving home. Let's not point out that he would also encourage some of them to go buy *more* beer when *they* ran out. I affectionately referred to these pants as his 'clown pants' because he could stuff so much in them and once in a while he would surprise me at the interesting things he would pull out of the numerous, and enormous pockets.

I don't recall how he got to most of these parties, but after a while, I started giving Jack rides home as he lived fairly close to me. We would talk about the people at the parties all the way home and laugh hysterically at the tricks he pulled on them. We called each other 'laughing buddies'. One night I didn't have a car for some reason and he ended up taking *me* home. He kissed me good-bye on the cheek when I got out of the truck. It was surprisingly exciting and completely unexpected. I don't think I slept that night wondering what that tiny, but very deliberate and nervously given peck on the cheek meant, exactly.

Jack and I dated for about two and a half years after that. We loved each other so intensely and so passionately, but we fought with just as much energy, if not more. We had both come from fairly abusive families so

I suppose we were just acting the only way we knew how.

Our arguments included physical fighting more often than not, and were mostly based on unfounded and imaginary alcohol induced jealousy on his part. I think my parents bought the story of a bird hitting my windshield the first time I came home with it smashed, but they were smart enough not to buy it the second time I tried to use the same story.

Friends would often try to encourage me to break up with him when they saw the bruises on my arms on a regular basis, but they didn't understand how bad he felt for doing it, or how much he loved me when he *wasn't* hitting me. They also didn't know that I got a few good punches in too, and once in a great while, I purposely picked a fight for lord only knows why. One thing that people don't often know or realize about battered women, is sometimes the seemingly violent situation they are in is truly the lesser of two evils *they think* they have to choose from.

When my brother or I were bad growing up, we got the belt or a stiff backhand from Dad; Mom would just pull half our hair out. Mom did try to get more creative with punishment, but it rarely worked. For the most part, their physical methods were pretty effective and I don't fault them at all for using them. My younger sisters never really got to experience the joy of the belt, as they were actually pretty good kids (maybe learning from me and my brother's mistakes). However, when my brother turned about 15, that's when things started to really get interesting.

To say my brother had a temper is like saying Mother Teresa was a nice lady. My brother would get mad because his go-cart or dirt bike didn't work and throw a wrench at the first person who made the horrible mistake of saying, "Hey, whatchya doin?" If I went crying to Mom and Dad with blood gushing out of my head, they would respond with, "Well, why did you make your brother mad?" Or "If you kids want to fight, pay for your own God Damn hospital bills," while promptly walking away, leaving you to figure out how to patch the hole in your head or gash in your limb. Unlike the beatings with the belt from Dad, that were often deserved, this 'behavior' from my brother didn't go over as well with me.

Getting back to Jack; when he and I fought, he would *just* punch me in the arms or the stomach. He never drew blood and never hit me in the face, whereas my face or head was my brother's *main* target. It was easy to rationalize, at 17 years old, that Jack loved me much more than my family did. Jack would bawl his head off because he felt bad after hurting me, whereas there were never any apologies at home—only clear warnings to stay away from my brother when he got mad. I heard "that's what you get for making him mad" more often than I could count.

One time my brother and I got into a pretty big doozy of a fight which resulted in some face and neck bruising as well as bleeding from the head (only *my* face, neck and head, of course) and I decided to call the police. Our parents weren't home and I knew I was risking pissing them off when they found out that I called the cops on their beloved only son, but I felt brave for some reason and did it anyway. Little did I know when I made the call, that there was no reason to worry about my parents even finding out.

Two police officers came to the house and asked a few questions. They didn't really seem to care much about what we were fighting about or the blood spewing from my head. They asked my brother how old he was. He said he was 16. They asked me how old I was. I said I was 18. Without any further discussion, one of the cops told me that since I was 18 years old, *I* didn't need to be there, and if *I* wasn't there, *this* wouldn't have happened.

I thought for sure that too much blood had drained from the gash in my head that I didn't hear him correctly until he made it more than clear by escorting me to my car to leave, even though I lived there at the time. I went to Jack's house—and I felt loved.

Pahrump was pretty spread out so it wasn't easy to just go to another friend's house for help and they would always be busy with their other friends anyway. No teenager or young adult wants to play hero and rescue you from a situation like that, and what do they know anyway? They are too busy trying not to get caught doing whatever *they* are doing wrong.

It's times like these when you really start to feel alone—like the whole world is cruising along minding its own business and you're just stuck on the side of the road—not even thumbing it, 'cause, hell, where would you thumb it to? I can remember watching the night sky in Nevada—the only thing it had in common with Minnesota—and thinking, "What am I doing here? Is this really *my* life?" Sometimes I thought for sure I was in an episode of the Twilight Zone, and "I" didn't even exist.

One thing that did feel real was fighting with Jack. There was one public fight between he and I that stands out. We were getting pretty physical in front of the only gas station in town and Kevin drove up. I didn't know Kevin very well; he was the older brother of my brother's best friend. Anyway, he got out of his car, walked over to Jack and said, "You want to beat on someone—be a man and beat on me instead of her." Now, you often hear of this scenario ending with the battered woman turning on the would-be-hero and taking her man's side. Not me! I grabbed that window of opportunity, ran to my car and drove off! Kevin was my hero that night and I will never forget him for doing that.

In a small town you may not know *every* kid, but you are never more than six degrees from any other kid, especially when there are multiple siblings—and because there were a few families with 10+ kids, it was hard not to be connected to everyone in some way or another.

One time 'the community' tried to get involved with Jack and me. It was far less effective than the incident with Kevin, and later it would become laughable. I was at my friend Laura's house and Mrs. Matthews was there visiting Laura's Mom. Mrs. Matthews didn't know me, or so I thought, but she said to me, "I know Jack hits you. You should stay away from him. I know those Nelson boys, they are nothing but trouble, and they always will be." I dismissed her words—just as a know-it-all teenager would. *I knew* she didn't know what she was talking about. *I knew* she didn't know how much Jack loved me and how remorseful he was after we fought. That remorse made a lot of difference in my book. Hell, it made *all* the difference. It made him real to me—it made his love real to me. The love he had for me *most* of the time more than canceled out the *moments* of madness.

Mrs. Matthew's middle daughter Olivia, would later turn down an engagement from a good Mormon boy

(Laura's older brother), to instead marry Jack's older brother Peter, the middle Nelson boy. They had a few kids and as far as I know, they are still together. After Jack and I broke up, *he* would marry Mrs. Matthews' youngest daughter, Quinnie, who once dated my brother. Jack and Quinnie would have a child together, and then she would later marry a guy that I also once dated. So the totally laughable part is this concerned Mother warned me to stay away from the very same boys that two of her three daughters would later marry and have kids with. Funny how that goes, isn't it?

But then in the small town of Pahrump, where we had a teacher who did some time for sexual assault, another teacher who married a former student who graduated a year early for the sole purpose of marrying *someone else*, this wasn't really that surprising or unusual at all. Small towns—I'll tell ya. Who needs cable, when you got a small town?

But let's get back to Jack. What was so great about him? I guess I kind of made the mistake of jumping the gun and explained why I would love him about three paragraphs back…If you like that explanation, you can skip this one—how's that for an author? Go ahead, skip on over this part, she says!

So anyway—why would I love someone that hit me when we fought? Well, for one, it was pretty rare that our fights were just *him* hitting *me*. Remember, violent fighting was a norm for my family and in Jack's case; it was much less violent than I was used to. Sadly, the love I got from Jack was so much more than I ever had in my life at that point that it made him attractive. Besides that, we didn't fight *constantly*, and making up does have its perks.

We actually had a lot of fun most of the time. We took a lot of drives in the desert, not really to 'mess around' as much as to just *see* what was *out* there. His family had lived there forever and being a native of the area, he knew a lot of little or unknown areas. He loved showing me cool places and he would often make up stories about the geography or plants that I would usually buy hook, line, and sinker. We would later have good laughs about how gullible I was.

We drove up to Mt. Charleston one time and he said, "You see that wall of rock there that has all those holes in it? Do you know what causes those holes?" I shook my head to indicate I had no clue, to which he responded, "Rock Termites. They burrow in the rocks and live in them. They work all winter making little tunnels so they can survive the hot summers in there." Yup, I bought that stupid shit! He actually didn't tell me it was a fib until years later when he heard me telling someone *else* all about Rock Termites.

One time we were out in Armargosa just exploring with my youngest sister for the day and she had to pee. She was very young, but yet was old enough to throw a fit about the fact that she was going to have to just use the side of the road. She squealed that she had to go so bad, but there was no restroom for miles. We both tried to 'educate' her about squatting, but she was just too freaked about getting pee on her. Jack came up with this idea that we would both hold her up somehow in a position that would keep her legs out of the stream of urine.

We each held her by an arm and a leg so her legs were spread slightly apart and straight out in front of her. This was the only way she was *sure* she would not get any on her legs and safely pee straight down. It was a good idea in theory. When she finally let it rip, it actually flew like a fountain over and on top of her legs instead of going straight down. Jack had initially looked away out of respect and decency but when he heard my "HOLY SHIT" followed by her screams clearly indicating this plan had gone all wrong, he turned around and we were all laughing so hard we nearly dropped her.

We had about 50 silly little nick names for each other and he would draw things for me constantly to represent the funny characters of how I made him feel. One of my favorites was a moose with a million points on his rack; under the drawing he wrote (much to the frowning of my parents when I hung it on my bedroom wall): "I'm horny as a moose." That became our little inside joke—when we were feeling frisky we would say, 'I'm feeling moosey." To this day, I can't look at any moose picture or stuffed moose toy without one of those memories popping up in my head.

I don't remember us ever talking about or planning a long-term future yet we must have because I bought him a wedding band. I think I paid $10 for it at Kmart. I slipped it on his finger under the table when we were having dinner at Nevada Palace in Las Vegas.

The ring ended up flying out the window of my truck during a fight somewhere by Wild West Casino in Pahrump just weeks later. There were many gifts that took flight out car windows during our relationship. He once bought me these really neat flowers with lights in them and during a heated argument; he threw them out the car window.

I loved them so much that I pulled over and we looked for them for at least 30 minutes. The only reason we gave up was because I stepped on a piece of glass which went through my shoe and I was bleeding. I actually tried to look for them another time by myself but to no avail. Why, oh why were those stupid flowers with lights in them so important? Who knows? Maybe because they were a symbol of the love that I knew was real.

One of my very fondest memories was the night we slept in the Ice House. The Ice House was a very old building in down town Las Vegas. Ice blocks were actually made there years ago and then loaded on trains to be shipped out to wherever ice goes. Jack's Dad had managed to buy the salvage rights to the place and had an RV inside so they could stay in town when they worked in there tearing apart the pipes and such.

One night me, Jack, and my brother went to Vegas for the hell of it. I think we had $5 total to our names. Jack decided it was a good idea to spend it all on Grolsh Beer—once we found someone over 21 to buy it for us, of course. Then we went to the Ice House. It was crawling with homeless people outside. I don't know if my brother slept at all that night, but Jack and I sure didn't. I was scared out of my mind, and he was feeling way too moosey but couldn't bring himself to make a move with my brother right across from us in the RV.

The next morning we were starving and had no money. For some reason, the one hour drive home seemed entirely too torturous to make without food, so Jack decided to take a lesson from the bums we just slept nearby and panhandled for money. Outside a 7-11 on Rainbow Blvd, the first lady he asked money from (saying it was for gas to get home) gave him $5, which we promptly spent on junk food right there at the 7-11 the second she pulled away.

Jack worked for his Dad on the mountain. His aunts actually lived on the mountain and hunted their own food. (That didn't stop them from going crazy when Jack or his family brought them up a pie from town.) They did a lot of dozing and clearing of the land, for some reason, I don't remember. I imagined they planned to grow something, someday.

When my Mom threw me out of the house when I was 17 for calling my sister a Bitch (which she was), I moved in with a couple that I was already babysitting for. I then babysat in exchange for rent and continued to go to high school. I also worked a few hours after school in a government type program job I got because we were a low-income family.

Jack would come by almost every night while I was babysitting and we pretty much played house. It honestly wasn't really because we *wanted* to play parents, per se, but because the couple that were the parents of the kid I babysat, were total fuck-ups and spent all their money partying. They actually thought it was ok for the kid to eat hot dogs *every single night* for dinner. Jack would spend the few bucks he earned most days working for his Dad on *real* food (we ate tacos a lot... Hey, we were still kids then too).

One night I was suffering with a horrible earache. I called Jack and he drove all the way to the store in the middle of the night to bring me medicine. He was very compassionate and thoughtful most of the time and he had an amazing sense of humor that kept a smile on my face—unless we were fighting over stupid shit of course!

No Safe Bets

After about six months I moved back home, and my brother and I formed a very brief union, informing our parents that he and I were moving to Las Vegas. Our argument was that there was just no future for us in Pahrump. My parents must have had their fill of that poe-dunk town as well because we all moved to Henderson, a neighboring city of Las Vegas, soon thereafter. This move added about an hour to my Dad's already more than an hour commute, but we finally made it to a big city where we could expand our horizons.

My brother continued to be an abusive asshole and Jack and I saw each other once in a while until he married Mrs. Matthews' youngest daughter (the same Mother who told me to stay away from him). I started dating someone who was the sweetest guy I had ever met, but I also thought he was *weird* for being so sweet. I just didn't know how to be treated like that and I had no idea how to act. Through my inability to understand how and why he could be so nice, I was thoughtless and inadvertently mean to him. He finally lost interest. Wrecking his car might have had something to do with our break-up as well.

I dated a few people here and there but nothing worth searching my brain for memories about. I was 19 when I met Rob one night while I was out with my best friend. It was just after they raised the drinking age to 21, but since we were going to a little neighborhood bar, we knew if we arrived just before the bouncer got there we could get in before they started carding people at the door.

Rob walked in and my friend flipped out; it was obvious she was in love with him. She was in love with *everyone* who was halfway good looking. She had a habit of staking her claim on the top three cutest guys in any place we went, making them off limits for me. I didn't really mind because I wasn't terribly interested in relationships at that time. But she was nuts over Rob; more than anyone else I had ever seen her take an interest in.

She said that he had gone away in the military so she was clearly thrilled to see him back. She called him over to our table and he sat by me. She was acting absolutely coo-coo over him. I thought he was cute, but couldn't see justifying the coo-coo behavior. They danced, we danced, and we chatted a bit; nothing special.

My best friend and I would run into him from time to time at different bars over the next year or so until we ran into him at the Harvest Festival in Pahrump. The

Pahrump Harvest Festival used to be a pretty big deal but I am not even sure if they even *have* the event anymore.

My friend and I were walking across the park and there was Rob with his t-shirt off and wrapped around his head to cover his melon from the heat. He looked ridiculous. Again, she went nuts over him and I stood off in the distance slightly embarrassed for both of them. He asked what our plans were later and my friend invited him to our ajoining hotel rooms to party later. "Great, another night of her gushing over him," I thought (eye roll).

By the time Rob showed up, my friend had already lassoed herself a really cute cowboy; she was big on the tight wrangler jeans look. Rob had cleaned up nicely, to my surprise, and because my friend was busy thinking up hog-tying ideas to try on her newfound cowboy, she didn't pay any attention to the attention Rob was paying to me. I loved my friend and cherished our friendship dearly, so *I was* paying a lot of attention to how much attention Rob was paying me.

I waited until it was blatantly clear (he kissed me), that he was indeed interested in me before I approached my friend with this development. I told her that her friendship meant more to me than anything and knowing how she felt about Rob, I would gladly reject his advances if that was her wish. She was pretty 'self-medicated' and had more than an 8 second hold on her cowboy, so she gave me a very clear green light with Rob.

The green light turned to a solid red the next morning when Rob was still there and her cowboy had ridden off into the sunset while she was sleeping. I was fairly surprised myself that Rob had not made a mad dash for the door before the sun came up.

Because he was still there, I was just sort of pacing, busying myself, mentally preparing for him to bolt, but then he started asking questions like, "How did everyone get there? Who drove?" I said I drove my car. He asked me to ride home, to Henderson, with him. I said I couldn't because I had my car. He said, "Let your friend drive your car home and you ride with me." Um... okay. So, I rode with Rob back to Henderson, which is about 80 miles or so from Pahrump.

We held hands the whole way home and I think I may have even sat next to him in the bench front seat. I had him drop me off at my friend's house so I could get my car.

He asked me for my phone number and said he would call me later. I had heard that before. I really wasn't holding much hope with him at all so when he asked where I lived, I was purposely vague because I didn't want to sit around going crazy waiting and wondering if he would ever stop by.

He gave me a quick, but nice, kiss goodbye and I got out of the car. I hung around at my friend's house a minute or two before heading home.

I lived with my parents off and on between the ages of 17 and 20 depending on fighting patterns with my brother and one of my sisters. During this short window of time, I was living at home. I went there to crash, as I was so tired from the crazy party filled weekend. I wasn't asleep five minutes when my brother frantically woke me up. "Teresa, there is a guy here to see you.... And he is good looking."

I honestly had no clue who it could be. It had not been more than 30 minutes since Rob dropped me off at my friend's house, yet there he was, standing in my parent's driveway. He said he just wanted to see me again, and take me out to dinner. Hmm imagine that, I thought.

He lived with his Mom at the time and she was on vacation, so I spent the better part of the next two weeks at his (Mom's) place. We got along great, but I was still leery of any sort of permanence for some reason. One night we were lying on the couch and he kept going on and on complaining about his job and how they were treating him. I snapped and said, "You are 23 years old—if you don't want to work there; DON'T!" And then I left. That somehow meant we were broke up.

I have always worked since I was 13 and I have done everything from bussing tables, to shoveling horse shit, to painting picnic tables, to warehouse work, to being a desk jockey, and if there is one thing I have always felt strong about, it's this: 'When there is more shit than shine, get out of that line'! Of course, no job is ever perfect and there will always be bad days, but when someone is tearing you down, personally, day after day.... You just simply must leave. There are other jobs and ways to earn a living, especially when you're young and don't have, or need much.

I kind of did that same thing with Ivan, my first high school boyfriend, where we dated for about a month and then I got cold feet and broke up, only to try to get back together again. I am sure there is some psychology there. I would guess it has to do with me feeling in control of the relationship, as in it either exists or doesn't exist as a direct result of my choosing. (There were probably some commitment issues, as well as just pure fear at work also.)

Well, after about a month of Rob and me not seeing each other, I missed him and sort of stalked him a bit (though no one referred to it as such back then). I left notes on his car, messages at work, etc. Somehow, we got back together and moved into an apartment together. It was a shithole infested with cockroaches that kept me up half the night flipping the lights on and off to hunt and kill them—but it was ours.

***

Rob and I fought occasionally but it was rarely very *bad* and we always made up quickly. I think I was able to fall for Rob initially because he wasn't that *bad* like Jack, but he wasn't that *good* like the super sweet guy I dated after Jack either; he was right in the middle. A safe bet, you could say.

We both had jobs and made about the same amount of money; about $8 an hour our first few years. We split the bills down the middle and filled our apartment with hand-me-downs and bargains from Pick-N-Save, which later became Big Lots I think. I will never forget our first official BRAND NEW purchase that we made together. It was a hanging wicker shaded lamp that we got at Lamps Plus on clearance for $20. We were so proud of buying something together, and in a *nice store* at that!

We had a hide-a-bed couch that was as heavy as a VW and the fabric on the arms didn't match the seat cushions. I am not sure why or where we even got it from, but I remember we paid $50 for it. Rob had a cheap trunk from K-Mart, which we used as our coffee table, and cheap plastic end tables that we got from Skaggs/Osco, which became Longs Drugs or something, for $5 each.

Our 13-inch TV was given to us by my parents. The volume didn't work so we had to sit right in front of it to hear anything. Rob had bought a bed from Salvation Army for $100. I thought $100 was ridiculous for it, but what did I know? I don't remember where we got our kitchen table set, but I know it was from a friend and it was cheap.

I was at work one day filing super important records when Rob walked in and announced that he just won $800 gambling. I was pretty excited, as that was a ton of money to us then. He wanted to march right down to the store and buy a REAL TV. We bought a really nice 27 inch (that was big then) JVC TV.

We ordered pizza delivery with the last $20 of the winnings and were sitting on the living room floor figuring out how to hook our VCR back up to it when someone knocked at the door. It was about 9:00pm so I couldn't imagine who it might be. I was quite taken back when I saw a miniature vampire at the door. It took me more than a moment to remember it was Halloween, but less than a second to realize we had no candy. I grabbed a Weight Watchers treat from the freezer and gave it to the little vampire; he can now *count* calories instead of Count Dracula (har, har, I crack myself up).

In the years that followed, Rob gambled more and more, though he usually hid it from me pretty well. One day after work he lost $400. Since that was half a month's salary to us back then, it was not as easy to hide. It hurt, both emotionally and financially—I reacted by saying I couldn't deal with someone so irresponsible. I was fed up with both the gambling and the occasional 'jamming out at his a-hole friend's garage on drinking and pot smoking marathons.' I packed my things to leave. Rob responded by grabbing my arms, pushing me against the wall and begging me not to go. That was the *only* time Rob ever laid hands on me. I was shocked—but I stayed. He never touched me or spoke to me like that again.

The funny thing about Rob and his lack of temper, despite that one incident, is that he totally cured mine. In my family, if you fought, you did so in a violent manner, often until blood was drawn (and it was usually mine). Throwing, breaking, and smashing things were as much a part of fighting as using a fork and spoon is to eating.

One afternoon I was trying to fight with Rob about who knows what, and he just wasn't 'playing along'. He was busy watching TV and ignoring me as I continued to raise my decibels in an effort to be 'heard'.

Finally, I went over to the bedroom door, grabbed each side of the doorknob, and in one quick upright jerking motion, yanked that sucker right off the doorframe. I looked over at Rob and waited for him to throw or break something, as this is how I was used to arguments progressing growing up.

He calmly looked away from the TV toward me and said in a completely normal tone of voice, "Now you have to fix that. I will loan you my tools but I am not helping you. You are not calling maintenance to do it for you; you have to fix it yourself." I did fix it myself, and I have never had another violent episode like that again. I felt really ridiculous and small for behaving that way and I truly thank him for that lesson.

Rob was a very hard worker with *big* dreams of being promoted from meat packer to meat cutter someday. After being a model employee at the same place for 11 years, and actually performing the job of a meat cutter (with meat packer pay) a good portion of the time, his hopeful promotion was nowhere in sight.

He was also very mechanically inclined and was talented in many areas of construction. What he didn't know, he would get a book and learn about it. He could take a book about how to rebuild a jet engine into the bathroom and come out an hour later, set the book down, and do it without referring back to the book or any other knowledge source.

He sat in front of a piano once, hit a couple keys and then played part of a song that was very familiar. I said, "I didn't know you could play the piano." He said, "I didn't either." It was the first time he tried. He could do that with about any instrument; test a few keys/strings/ whatever and 'get it'. In many ways, he was literally a genius but never had any drive to use his true talents for financial gain.

Because he really was a pretty great guy, and I wasn't too shabby myself, we decided to get married. We had stopped in the Candlelight Chapel next to the Rivera and across from Circus Circus in Las Vegas just because we liked how it *looked* like a church, but obviously wasn't one. I grew up Catholic and he grew up Mormon but neither of us cared for organized religion now that we could think for ourselves.

Although the idea of having a reception with friends and family and a giant pot luck like we used to have back home in the basement of the church at every wedding or funeral sounded nostalgic, I preferred it to be just us. Yes, *I wanted* to go down to the chapel, in my sweats, and him in his jeans and just do it—just us—in the eyes of whatever ordained person was on shift that day—and it just be the two of us. *He said* his family would never forgive him if he did that so they would have to at least be there. Well, there went the notion I could wear my sweats then.

Once you throw out the hope you can get married in your sweats (yeah, I'm not your typical girl in case you haven't figured that out yet), the details involved in wedding planning just start to snowball into an avalanche of bullshit. Finding a dress I don't hate, renting tuxes, picking the right wording for invitations, the right color and kind of flowers, renting a hall, tables, chairs, food serving crap, figuring out some sort of center pieces, securing a DJ, a photographer, having a cake made, oh and don't forget the topper for the cake!

Believe it or not that was the one thing that I gave up on; I looked and looked and looked for a topper I liked and finally said, "Yeah, the cake is going topless." My sister actually borrowed one from a friend and slapped it on top at the last minute. I had reached an "I'm tired of trying to please everyone and do what everyone *else* thinks I should, I don't care anymore" attitude.

Being the rebel that I am, I *did* put my foot down about one thing. At that point I had seriously had enough of doing what everyone *else* thought I should. I've always thought the smashing cake in each other's face was just stupid. It's not only dumb, but messy and degrading. Completely pointless! I had done pretty much all of the wedding preparation for the wedding *he* thought *his* family would expect (I'm not bitter or anything), so I asked Rob for that *one* thing. I asked Rob to please tell the DJ that we are just going to cut the cake and serve it to people. We are *not* going to smash it in each other's faces.

So at the appropriate time, as if on cue, the DJ announced the cake was about to be cut. We were both visiting with friends and family in separate parts of the hall and as instructed, we met back at the cake. Through my gritted smile as people snapped pictures, I asked Rob if he remembered to tell the DJ we are not ruining two good pieces of cake for other people's 'expectations' and sick traditional pleasure. Through *his* tooth gritted smile he mumbled 'no, sorry, I forgot.' Had I had the knife in my hand instead of the useless-as-a-murder-weapon triangular pie thingy, I would have stabbed him to death right there. Okay, maybe not; but I was pissed. It was the *one* thing I wanted to make *my own* decision on, damn it!

***

Funny side note: That Candlelight Chapel where we got married? They moved it to build something (in true blow-it-up-and-build-something-bigger/better-Vegas style). Well, guess *where* they moved it? The Clark County Museum. Yah... I don't feel old at all now that the place I got married is part of a FUCKING MUSUEM!

***

We had spent a lot more than we could afford on the wedding (to please everyone else. Again, I'm not bitter or anything) so we decided to move in with my parents (and two younger sisters) to save money to buy a house. If you ever want incentive to save money, move in with family! We fought about the most ridiculous things.

50

Rob got yelled at once for putting the butter away (if you refrigerate it, it gets hard and it is too *difficult* to spread on toast, which was a staple in our house).

One of my sisters drove us to the decision to get a hotel room one night over a fight about us buying toothpaste *'when we should just be using theirs so we could save more money to buy our own house and get out'*. We could have bought about 20 tubes of premium toothpaste with the money the hotel room cost us, but our sanity somehow seemed like a good investment at the moment. Ironically, of all places, we decided it would be 'fun' to stay at Circus Circus, right across the street from where we got married.

During that first year, we were also feuding with his family over pictures. Rob and I paid for our own wedding. Even though we scrimped on so much, got great deals, and did as much as we could ourselves; it still cost about $3,500, which was a lot when we were only making about $10 an hour. We got about $700 in cash for wedding gifts which ultimately determined where or how far we could go on our honeymoon.

We got a great deal on the photographer. She let us have the negatives (pre-digital days) which was awesome. I had tons of copies made myself, including enlargements, for any picture his family was in, and just gave them to them. Remember that part about me *giving* the pictures to them because what happened next took years and a few therapy sessions to get over.

We were married in May. About a month or two after our wedding, we got a call from Rob's sister saying she wanted to get all the kids together. Okay, great. They wanted to plan their Mom's 50th birthday BBQ. Okay, odd. I thought something was fishy right away because there isn't much to 'plan' about a BBQ that couldn't be done over the phone.

After some inquiring and prodding it came out: first, they wanted to get all the kids together for a family portrait and they wanted to *coordinate* how everyone would dress for this family photo. One of Rob's sisters' informed him that they were wearing fall colors and that the girls had already picked out blouses. (The truth was *she* picked out and bought the blouses, just different fall shades, and told the girls that's what they were wearing, and of course let them know what they owed her.) She wanted to make sure Rob and his brother coordinated, *not clashed,* with the girls' blouses (major eye roll). At least the picture was going to be FREE since they had an offer for a complimentary 8x10 from Olin Mills. And it being FREE was a big deal to us at the time—and it would have been to you too, had you been living with my one sister.

Second, the surprise birthday party went from being a simple backyard BBQ to a major event, including renting a hall, ordering a fully catered meal, fancy invitations, a DJ, and a professional photographer to document it all. Suddenly that big FREE balloon which looked so nice and promising popped in our faces. I gave Rob a glance and he gave me one back, and we were both thinking the same thing: his uppity sisters were trying to out-do our wedding by making their party a bigger and better bash—and making sure our wedding picture got replaced by theirs because apparently ours had no place on anyone's wall or mantle.

The *free* 8x10 turned into a giant wall size photo *and* also into a packet of photos for each of the five kids; each sibling was told they owed $60 for their packet, whether they wanted it or not (who the hell are you going to give *nine wallet pictures* of grown adults to?).

So now that they were demanding cash for pictures that started out 'free', we started wondering how much they were going to ask us to contribute for this birthday party. The 'magic number' came soon enough; $200 from each family member. His sister knew we were still recovering from the cost of our wedding, so we thought it was a pretty big *dig* when she said, "I have five *GRAND* set aside to spend on this party, with or without your help."

In the end, it turned into a full-on family feud where horrible things were said including, *"Rob didn't love his mother because he wasn't willing to pay for these pictures and chip in $200 for the party."* What kind of a person says something like that? But this whole farce didn't even stop there. The final show down was based on who would get *Mom* the best gift. This whole thing started ugly and just got uglier at every turn.

We never received an invitation to Rob's Mother's birthday party but we knew when it was and purposely made ourselves busy working on home improvement projects that day. Rob's sister came by that afternoon with her bags packed for the biggest guilt trip ever. She scolded Rob for not wanting to go to his Mother's party. He tried to say he didn't know about it because he wasn't invited. His sister looked over at me, then back at Rob and said so softly that it was almost sappy, "YOU are invited, and YOU are more than welcome to come." I tilted my head and thought to myself, 'Gee, I don't think she likes me.'

BONUS: Editor's WTF? Q & A with the author

Editor: How did you determine to marry Rob? Was it just a natural consequence of living together?

Author: Yeah, pretty much I guess...other than the gambling and pot smoking, he was a great guy and we got a long super. Also, the ONE TIME I tried to 'run back home to Mom and Dad'...they pretty much TOLD ME to go back to him and that I couldn't do any better...ya, no shit! I actually yelled at them and said 'you know... if HE came and told you that "I" was smoking pot...you would probably tell HIM to leave ME!.. They didn't say anything to that. They knew I was right. I never felt like my parents liked me very much.

Editor: Was there any pressure to do so? Did he ask you? Did you ask him? Did it just come up all by itself?

Author: I got tired of waiting for him to ask, so I asked him while we happened to be passing each other in the kitchen; Yup, super romantic - right in front of the golden yellow fridge – "Will you marry me?" "Sure," he says. Then he went back to the couch to watch TV. I picked out my ring at Montgomery Wards (don't laugh) and made all the layaway payments myself. He didn't seem to mind as long as I wasn't snooping in his side of the financials to notice he was still gambling.

Editor: Was there any fear of the big step you were about to take?

Author: No. But, Oh my God, I just remembered; the night *before* the wedding he was at his loser friend's house BBQ-ing the meat for our reception and I went over there to check on him (to see if he needed any help). One of the wives said 'oh, they went down to the 'titty bar'. This would have been like his fucking 3rd bachelor party. I didn't care about the girls though—what I cared about was that he had our honeymoon money in his wallet. Yep, sure as shit, I walked in there and he had his back to the boobies and was throwing *our honeymoon* money away in the machines. I dragged him out by his ear (literally), and had a bit of a temper relapse that night. I actually kicked a hole in the dash of the car (that I had to sit a certain way the next day to hide in the wedding photos). We ended up staying up that whole night fighting and I actually swallowed a shit ton of diet pills; dumb, I know. Soooo, after fighting all night, we went and had a 99 cent breakfast at the Rainbow Casino and parted ways to 'get ready to get married'. At the ceremony, I kept scratching my chest which shows up in some of the pictures. Rob was a total ham and *sang* his vows to me which of course everyone loved him for because he was suuuuuch a charmer (I wanted to either barf or kick him in the balls for looking so good after what we had been thru the night before).

Editor: Did you take vows? How many people were there? What was your Mother and Father's reaction? Did you have a 'wedding party'—like bridesmaids/best man, etc.?

Author: Yes, just the vows the minister told us to say. It was a small chapel so not many people, maybe 50 at the most. My Dad walked me down the aisle—it was 'ok'—nothing 'bonding' or 'special' or anything. I purposely didn't invite my brother though; he was (still is) unpredictably violent at times. He had a class for work that day that he couldn't miss anyway. He showed up at the reception with jeans/t-shirt on for our 'family picture'.

There is an interesting story about my Maid of Honor. It was the same best friend who initially was so googoo over him. Well she and I had a falling out over an entertainment center that Rob and I built for her. The agreement was that she bought the materials and would 'help'. We had to use another friend's garage to build it in since we lived in a tiny apartment, so we had to drive over there and inconvenience them every time we wanted to work on it. My *best* friend only showed up one time to 'help'—and she showed up in her bathing suit to lay out and get a tan while *we* worked on it, so when it was done, we asked her for a whopping $50 in labor (which barely covered our gas going back and forth to get materials and work on it). Mind you, it started small but then she realized she wouldn't be able to see it over her waterbed (yes, I am dating myself) we had to add a whole additional bottom piece to it. Anyway, we ended up giving her the money she had in it for materials and keeping it ourselves. Rob was a pretty easy going guy so it surprised me a little when he said he would rather set it on fire than give it to her. This ordeal ended her and I's friendship.

So how did she still end up being my Maid of Honor? Well, *he* wanted a best man. *I* didn't want anyone there but just him and I alone, but noooooooooo he had to have his family there which meant I had to have MY family there; then *he* wanted a his high school buddy to be his best man. Ok... NOW WHAT? Who the hell am I going to have on my side then? Well, a year had gone by of not talking to her but I couldn't imagine anyone else I would want to stand by me but my former best friend. So I called her and she said yes. We were friends again for a good long while until she hooked up with a stupid lazy dope head Mexican and started smoking meth.

Editor: Wow! I'm sure a lot of girls can relate to typical drama-filled girl fights, but I'm not sure how many end because they hooked up with a dope head Mexican and started smoking meth; interesting. Tell me more about your parents—they sort of hover in the background of your story but don't really appear too often in person— was that how it was in your life?

Author: Ya, all of us kids were pretty independent. We really didn't have Mom/Dad/family time. They were always working and Dad had an injury before I was born that prevented him from walking much—he couldn't even dance the whole father/daughter dance with me.

Editor: Also, your sister's animosity towards you is strange—when did you first notice it? Before or after the wedding? Why don't you think she liked you? Just one of those things?

Author: My one sister was always the odd one—like a middle child but she was the youngest for a long time. My youngest sister and I are 10 years apart—she was 'an accident'. She was the only one I think my Mom really loved. My brother and I were never good in school, but this sister was—so we hated her for making us look bad. We really don't like each other to this day. She always wants to 'hash things out' which is her speak for 'It's been a while, let's fight some more.'

Editor: I was actually meaning your sister-in-law...

Author: Oh, she was just an uppity bitch.

Comfort Food is a Killer

I gained 50 pounds the first year Rob and I were married. I think stress had a little to do with it. Going out to eat a lot to escape *my* family's house and the ringing phone of *his* family calling about bullshit drama also may have played a role.

We lived with my family about a year before we bought our house. We gutted our new place and re-did just about everything that could be re-done. We poured a slab and built a covered patio the full length of the back of the house and also built a block wall around the back yard. It was a lot of work, definitely a learning experience, it turned out great and it was ours.

We stayed pretty busy, but when things slowed down a bit, Rob started gambling again. At over $1,000 a pop a couple times, it took a toll on our relationship, not to mention our finances. I hurt my back at work and put on even more weight, which also drove us further apart. I was around 230 pounds then.

We bought a little boat and Rob started going fishing instead of gambling. He had a company truck at the time so the boat was permanently hitched to his personal truck. Nearly every day he would come home from work, get out of his company truck and jump straight into his personal truck to be on the lake in less than 15 minutes. This ritual also meant I had time to get home and relax before he came home again. Life was good. Or so it seemed.

Eventually I learned that Rob was gambling again and lying to me about it the whole time. I'm not sure what led him to return to gambling but it seemed he always found his way back into the casinos, which then led us back into debt. Now, Rob throwing our hard-earned money down the drain was one thing, but the lies were the ultimate betrayal.

After Christmas one year he announced that he was tired of not having money to buy gifts around the holidays—I agreed with this opinion and took it to mean he was going to try to curb his gambling habits! I didn't see it coming when he revealed his way of ensuring we had money for Christmas presents next year was signing us up for a "Christmas Club Account" (think Columbia Record Club, just in reverse). He informed me that the bank would be taking $50 out of our checking account each month and moving it into a *super-secret untouchable vault*, which we couldn't access until sometime just before Christmas the following year. I informed him that was a stupid idea because it probably paid little or no interest and most likely had penalties if we HAD to get it out early for some reason—but he laid it on pretty thick that he wanted to be able to get *me* something *special* next year. Of course, this shut me up.

I was in control of the checkbook and I noticed that they always pulled out an odd amount for this Christmas Club Account. Sometimes it was $49.75 and sometimes it was $46.23 or whatever...I didn't think too much of it. Then one day I bounced a check. Our balance was off—gee, how did that happen?— I was *pissed* off before I even called the bank (of course, I *knew* it was someone else's fault).

I phoned the bank while Rob was sitting with me at the kitchen table. He looked cool as a cucumber while I tried to figure out where I went wrong in my math, which led me to ask why they kept taking out different amounts for this "Christmas Club Account." I must have mentioned the name "Christmas Club Account" a half dozen times without the representative making any comments or corrections as Rob sat right there listening. Finally, after being completely irate with this poor woman and not getting anywhere, I hung up in frustration.

Eventually I realized there *never* was a Christmas Club Account, and instead what "we" had was a "Line of Credit" that Rob had pulled $1,500 out of to either gamble away or to repay personal gambling debts borrowed from friends; to be honest, I don't know which, and didn't much care anymore. That wasn't what struck me the most anyway.

What struck me most was the way he had just sat there and watched me—as though he were placidly plastered out of his mind—while I *argued* with this woman on the phone over a phony account, which *he* had claimed to set up! I was in awe that he could sit so easily and watch me look like a complete idiot—all because of a complete lie he told me *months* ago.

Believe it or not, that was when my heart began to break—a little sliver of a crack, somewhere in there where everything should have been honky-dory fine and solid because that is where you keep your trust in your lover... Like a little tiny crack in a sidewalk and up pops a weed—a weed that no matter what you spray on it, no matter how many times you pull it, it always seems to come back, as if to taunt you. Losing faith—losing trust. You always have to keep an eye on it. That, or throw out the lying bastard, er um, I mean dig up the cement and pour a thicker, better one.

Well, Rob had his tricks to try to "seal the cracks." One of them was to try to stuff gifts in the hole. One time he gave me a beautiful Amethyst ring for an anniversary present, which he made a big production of saying that he had been making payments on for some time from his pizza delivery tip money (a side job he got to pay off gambling debts).

A rather large argument about a week later led me to find a receipt in his wallet showing he had won $1,300 just days before our anniversary at a local casino. Of course, I asked him where the winning money was, to which he said, "I paid off the refrigerator and blew the rest."

Oh, really? I just got over the flu and gave birth to an Orangutan that looks like an alien version of Elvis eating a piece of toast that looks like it has Jesus' face burned in it. What...What? That didn't make sense to you?

We had bought a new refrigerator for about $900 about a year before *this little event*. I had written a check to pay it off at least 10 months prior so it seemed very strange when he said *he just* paid it off. And *blew* the rest? On *what*? Okay, let's deal with the first order of bullshit first.

"How could you pay off a refrigerator that was already paid off?" I asked. "I intercepted the check when you put it in the mailbox 10 months ago and withdrew the same amount of money so it would balance right in the checkbook," he tells me. OMG, my heart sunk! But then my thoughts started turning and I wondered out loud, "Then why didn't we get more statements for the remaining payments?" He cleverly explained, without any hint of remorse, "I took the statements out of the mail box before you came home and kept making the minimum payments [at 21% interest] each month with money orders."

OMFG! I felt the world spinning—I was on the verge of complete disbelief that he could carry on this bullshit for 10 months—and now stand here and 'fess up like it was something to be proud of! Here he was stacking new lie on new lie—a new one every single month.

So, "How did you *blow* the rest?" I asked, as if it even mattered at this point. "I knew I couldn't come home with the money because I would have to admit I gambled so I bet the rest [$800 or so] on one hand of blackjack." What?!?

"WHAT IF YOU ACTUALLY WON?

THEN WHAT?" I screamed.

"I purposely busted so I wouldn't."

Are you F'n kidding? I thought!

"Why didn't you just hand some random change lady all the money and say Merry F'n Christmas instead of paying the casino's power bills for Fuck sake?"

Well, that cool cucumber just looked at me like *I* was the one with the problem—can you beat that?

Over the years that followed there were *so many* "presents on layaway" or "deposits on trips" to explain why he pulled money off credit cards. Somehow, just before he would present these *neat* and *thoughtful* gifts, he would somehow let it slip but act like I found out and then say, since I *ruined* the surprise... He then would take my imaginary gift off the imaginary layaway or cancel the imaginary trip. Asking where the money went then was just pointless after a while, as the lies just got to be more and more ridiculous, and it became a waste of time to argue anymore.

Fourteen years later, it was up to $7,000 that he had taken off of our credit cards. I never, to this day, could figure out how he would go to work on time, and come home on time, not have time missing from his paycheck, but somehow have the time to gamble that much money. We lived in Portland, Oregon by then, and the most damage you could do without going to an Indian Casino was quarter video poker machines at the bars—so to blow $7,000 would take some serious time, I would think.

He never said he had a problem with my weight, but every now and then when I was frustrated and complained, he would suggest that I try to have some "control" with my eating. One day I finally replied, "I will tell you what, I will give you three quarters each day. I want you to take *one* quarter and put it in a video poker machine in the morning, then take another *one* and put it in at lunch, and then go back at dinner and put the final *one* in. No more—No less, and it must be three times a day that you manage *each* quarter." I could do it, but then I didn't have a gambling problem either.

I could control *anything* related to gambling or any other addictive *thing* for that matter; but food?—*that* was my drug of choice.

The thousands taken off our credit cards, at a ridiculous interest rate, not to mention stupid transaction fees, led me to get a financial separation. This was a neat little thing you could do in Oregon even if you're not ready to physically split up. I also didn't think we could *afford* to physically separate because of his gambling. I split all of our bills down the middle, which I thought was extremely generous given a large portion of *our* debt was *his* gambling. I mean, come on, I didn't eat *that* much!

Within three months, he had withdrawn another $13,000 off of, now *his*, credit cards. He must've been depressed as hell is all I can think of. I should know—when I was depressed I packed on the pounds like he was tacking on the debt.

I put all my energy into knocking down the balance on *my* side. I actually even managed to put some money away to leave if he didn't mend himself and do something about the crack in my heart that had now turned into a canyon. I swear, it was so big forest rangers could come and scope it out, people from East Coast suburbs could drive out with their families and pitch tents, and kayakers could go rafting down it when the winter snows thawed—that's how big it was! Yet still, I was hoping he would come out of it—and at least help me bridge it—but I knew deep down that if he hadn't stopped by now, 14 years into our relationship, he wasn't likely to any time soon.

One evening I just snapped. It wasn't a snap like Hoover Dam collapsing—it was more like the last straw on the camel's back—you know, *that* straw. I went to the bedroom and started stuffing a backpack with some clothes. "Where are you going?" He calmly asked. (He may have been calm because he had just got stoned with a friend of mine, who was also my supervisor at my job. I let her stay with us for a while because she caught her boyfriend screwing a stripper in his truck). "I don't know," I replied. He then thought a second, while he was forgetting to blink his eyes, which were getting as dry as his mouth. He then said, "When are you coming back?" I said, "I'm not. You're a loser and I am leaving." That was the end; as tranquil as the old folk's home after they pass out the meds and send them off to their nappy times.

Losing More than My Marriage

I went to a cheap hotel the night I left my husband and about an hour later, *she* called. I ignored the phone. My supervisor, who stayed at my house, even though I left, called more than a few times before stopping for the night. Rob did not call me once. As I laid there in the musty smelling room, I actually opened a Bible that was laying on the nightstand. There was a list of some sort that directed you to certain chapters and verses for whatever dilemma you might be facing at the time. I ran down the list and couldn't find one for "genius husbands who wasted their talents, gambled, lied, and smoked pot with their wife's supervisor," so I settled on "Marital Issues." I read the scriptures this list referred me to; it didn't help at all.

The next morning I went to work a bit early since I was pretty much up all night thinking anyway. (Never once did I think that I made the wrong decision by leaving however). I was sitting at my desk when my supervisor called my cell phone. I didn't answer. She kept calling and I kept ignoring it. Her desk was right behind mine in our bullpen office; I was going to see her soon enough. When she arrived, she walked past my desk and said, "You really should talk to Rob, he is worried about you." 'Hum, that's interesting...since HE IS NOT THE ONE CALLING ME, YOU ARE', I screamed silently in my head.

I got an apartment and asked Rob what I could take from our condo. He said I could have anything I wanted; so I took everything. I took his bed; I say "his" because we had been sleeping in separate rooms for the better part of the last two years before my supervisor needed a place to stay. I took the twin (my) bed that my supervisor was sleeping on then, the couch, the TV, the dishes, and both vacuum cleaners. I have no idea why we had two vacuum cleaners, but I thought I should take them both, just in case. Shortly after he arrived home that day, he called and calmly said, "Could you have at least left the couch so I have somewhere to sleep?" I replied just as calmly as he spoke to me, "I left the floor, didn't I?"

I wasn't really that hurt, bitter, or angry when I initially left, but I think the fact that he didn't call me at all, didn't try to work things out, in addition to having to sit next to my supervisor all day at work knowing she was still living with my husband, going home to him, probably getting stoned with him, talking about things *we* should have been talking about, just got to me. The only power I felt I had was to take everything. I did end up bringing back the twin bed, the couch, and one of the vacuums only a week later; so I'm not really *that* bad.

***

Living alone for the first time in my life, I discovered that I loved to be naked. I got up one Saturday morning, showered, started to put on my clothes and thought... Hum... I don't *need* to get dressed today at all. I sat on my kitchen chair—totally naked. I got food out of the fridge, and ate it—naked. I walked up and down the hall—naked. I flung out my arms, twirled around, and did a little jig, tapping my heels in the air—naked— okay, okay, maybe I didn't do *all* that—but, hey, you know what? *It felt great* to be totally naked!

***

The place where I worked was downsizing rapidly and it was less than comfortable working with my supervisor who continued to stay at my former residence with my husband. I was pretty sure they weren't screwing, but I honestly didn't care at that point. It was more about the shock of how little I apparently mattered to him, or to her for that matter, which really made me want to get out of there.

I called a consulting company that I had worked for before to ask if they had any work; anywhere. They said they had a contract job in Michigan. It was coming up on winter, and since I grew up in Minnesota, I was pretty sure what Michigan would be like. I asked if they had work anywhere else. They told me the salary and since it was about twice what I was currently earning, I quickly decided I could buy a warmer coat.

It was supposed to be a three-month contract. Everyone thought I was crazy for leaving a *permanent* job for a three-month job even though it paid double what I was currently earning. I explained to these people who clearly didn't understand, that there is no such thing as a *permanent* job, and in case they hadn't noticed, we were laying off more and more people every week. I told them not to worry their pretty little heads, I would be just fine.

The three-month job turned into almost a year-long gig. I actually didn't mind the winter at all and the changing seasons were nice. I was still eating for comfort. In mid-July, I tipped the scale (literally—that fucker buckled right under me—I guess those "capacity" stickers aren't kidding) at just over 300 pounds. When that summer's humidity hit, I was beyond *miserable*. I felt like a pig at the county fair, and the grocery chain reps are walking by looking at the blue ribbon I just won for "most bacon content."

When my manager announced we were ending our contract in three weeks, I was the only one in the group that nearly shouted for joy. I'd had enough of that humidity. I went back to the Portland area to stay with a friend. It'd been a year since I'd been gone. I felt it was time to get serious and start fresh again. That meant looking in the mirror—and trying to figure out how in the hell 300 pounds had happened.

Granted, I didn't feel *bad* about being fat. In fact, strange as it may sound, the only times I really felt fat was when the numbers on the scale said I was, when my plus size clothes kept getting tighter, and of course when my feet were screaming in pain every time I stood up.

But here I was back in Portland—and I was tired of *being* fat. I wanted to look the way I felt inside.

I took a break from job hunting and decided to do some more research on the gastric bypass surgery. I had tried to have the surgery a few times before but there was always a roadblock. I always had to attend classes first, which I would go through and then my employer would change insurance companies, or I wouldn't be able to get the time off work, or whatever. There was always *something*.

Now, I had the *time*—and besides, I reasoned, that if I didn't get a job *soon* I would have to file bankruptcy *anyway*, so why not throw some medical expenses in there too, what the hell? I know that doesn't sound ethical, but I also knew that if I *did* get a job, and I knew I would, that I would do the right thing and pay it all back.

I drove down to Las Vegas to attend a seminar by Dr. Whitgrove (real name-great guy) out of San Diego. He had done Carnie Wilson's (real name-maybe you've heard of her; she is also a wonderful soul) surgery as well as a friend of mine's. I attended the seminar and felt pretty comfortable with him so I proceeded to scheduling the surgery.

I made a cool little website about my upcoming surgery for the purpose of soliciting funds from friends, and anyone else for that matter. There just some nut job on a talk show that made a website announcing she was $80,000 in credit card debt from her shopping addiction. Through her website, she got enough donations to pay it all off. Wow, I thought, certainly if *she* could get people to give her $80,000 to pay off her shopping addiction, I could get $28,000 in donations to have a life altering surgery that would make me healthier and live longer, right?

I was certain that I had about 25-50 friends in my email list that would spend $10 to buy me lunch, so surely they would *love* to donate $10-$20 toward my surgery, right? And if they forwarded my email request to 10 of their friends, and so on, and so on... I might even get enough in donations to cover the plastic surgery I would later need to remove the extra skin after I lost all the weight? Right? Wrong!

I received a whopping $140. A $50 donation was from a friend of a friend—who immediately became *my* friend—and $70 from a former supervisor who hated me when I worked for him. Just in case you're not very good at math, that means I got $20 from just one other person out of the 50 or so I sent the email to *and* all those they forwarded it to—*if* they did, which now that I think about it, they probably didn't.

One little bonus I *did* get, however, was a sweet little lecture from a former supervisor saying she *would* help me out, but she was afraid if she did then it would make it *too easy* for me and I wouldn't try hard enough on my own. This, mind you, from a woman who received more help than I have ever seen from friends and co-workers every time her lying and cheating husband went on a gambling sprees, pawning everything from the computer she brought home from work, to her Franklin Covey Daily Journal (no shit). These 'events' were typically followed by a break-everything-in-sight temper tantrum when he got caught. The funny thing was, the first things he would break would be the very things that people loaned her to 'help her out'. So naturally, we all got used to the creative lies that followed as to how this stuff got stolen or broke. Sadly, it almost became entertaining among her staff. That is, to everyone *but* the person who loaned their shit to her, of course. One night at a cocktail party a few of us who worked with her were recounting all of the BS stories she told and how much people loaned her over the years. As a cap to the end of each story, Rob would sing parts of the song '[Life is just a] Fantasy' by Aldo Nova. It was hilarious.

Well, I wasn't about to let a silly little thing like finances, or the lack of supportive friends stop me from finally having this surgery. Like I said, there had always been roadblocks before, but this time I was hell bent and determined to change my appearance and get the real me out in plain sight! This was control, baby! I was taking my problem by the reigns come hell or high water!

The surgery was scheduled and I was mentally ready—then I got a call for a job back in Nevada. The job would have had insurance to cover it, but that would mean I would have to take 2-3 weeks off my first year there. I was determined to have my surgery, damn it, and the sooner the better. Besides, if I waited, I thought, there might be another wrench with insurance bullshit again, and I will be fat forever...

I explained the surgery situation in complete honesty to my future boss (including me not wanting to take the time off work for recovery so soon after starting). She said, go ahead and have the surgery, have a safe and speedy recovery, and start when you're ready. So I did, and I spent the next two years paying off $42,000 in credit card debt between the surgery and plastic surgeries to remove excess skin. I looked and felt amazing!

Sorta.

Life is Short – Play Naked

I kept journals of my weight loss progress and there were a few unexpected surprises along the way. First of all, I may have weighed 320 pounds when I had the surgery done, but you couldn't have *told me* I was fat—and you'll see what I mean later on. When I was 320 pounds, I was still cute, funny, smart, nice, a great friend, and I could *almost* keep up with the best of them (well, until my feet started hurting). I was always busy doing something. I was like a water buffalo—who calls a water buffalo fat? Nobody! They call 'em—large and in charge!

A friend once said to me, "Teresa, we can't keep up with you now, how will we ever keep up with you when you lose weight?" And that was a good question:

Wherever I traveled, I spent my time running around seeing everything the area had to offer. Now, my feet *did* always hurt and everyone within earshot was pretty much tired of hearing me complain about them. My feet hurt so much, that I had to keep tennis shoes by the bed and put them on just to go to the bathroom because the carpet floor was not enough cushion for my weight.

Despite the pain in my feet, I still didn't let it stop me from much. I often read about other heavy women and the way they talked about themselves: "I ballooned up to 200 pounds and I couldn't fit in a movie theater seat anymore," or, "I shot up to 190 and tried to go for a walk but a truck drove by and some guys yelled at me, 'Work that fat ass'."

I would scoff at these stories. Who ARE these people? I was over 300 and I fit in a movie theater seat just fine. I went to the movies all the time, and yes, even ate popcorn in public—*eeeeks!* I also walked a lot, and not once did anyone make a comment or yell out a truck window about my shape or size. I was never afraid to flirt with the cutest guy in a bar (or wherever I was). I figured if he wasn't interested, it must be because he didn't like fat girls. Oh well…. I don't like skinny guys either; NEXT! I didn't take too much personally when I was fat; I *knew* I was still awesome.

When I finally got under 200 pounds after my by-pass, I was pretty darn stoked. I was going through clothes as fast as could, and for the first time in a very long time I actually started enjoying shopping. I didn't allocate much money for new clothes—every spare cent went to pay off the credit cards from my surgeries. In fact, that became almost an obsession, seeing how much

I could pay on them and still have a little left for fun and travel (and shopping!).

The surprising thing was that as I lost weight, I began to get depressed. It was like someone had stripped me of my armored coat of confidence that I hid behind— that I clung to for so many years. I started having occasional anxiety attacks. It took me a while to figure out why.

One of two epiphanies happened a year after my surgery. I was celebrating by going to visit my uncle in San Diego where I had my surgery. We were in one of his favorite bars with his friends, a couple of which I had met a year prior when I was at my biggest. They were all happy to see the new me, but liked me just the same as when we met when I was fat. They were congratulatory, but not overly excited about my weight loss, which meant to me, that they saw the *real* me before—which I thought was pretty cool.

A girl with long black hair was standing next to my uncle at the bar. It was very crowded and she made it very clear that *she* needed more room. She kept swishing her hair on my uncle to get him to scoot more toward me and kept making rude faces at us, rolling her eyes as if we didn't belong there, and she did. I got up from my stool and was standing behind it so my uncle could scoot his stool in closer. This still wasn't enough for this woman.

My uncle got up to go to the bathroom and she immediately shoved his stool away from her and toward me. I had reached my limit with this bitch. I gently, but firmly, moved it back into its original spot. She gave me a look of death. I responded to her look with, "My uncle is coming back; he just went to the bathroom." Just then the group of friends she was with decided to leave. As she walked behind me, she hissed like a snake, *"Maybe if you would lose a few pounds we'd have more room."*

WHAT?… THE…? I was floored.

All I could think of at that moment to respond with was, "I would rather lose *you* instead." In the split second, I had visions of grabbing her by the hair, yanking her to the ground and pounding in her face right in front of all her yuppie friends. Lucky for her (and me) she kept walking. I'm not really a violent person (anymore). I hadn't been in a real fight since high school, but the last time I checked, we are still allowed the freedom of our own thoughts (but maybe I should check again—it's been a few days).

I was proud that I defended myself—but actually having to do so was such a foreign feeling. Everyone within earshot of her remark, including those who *knew* I had just dropped 140 pounds, had their mouths hanging open in astonishment. It took me only a moment to realize what just happened. Someone… *Someone*… just actually made a comment about my weight, for the first time *ever*. My brain was racing. Why? I looked fantastic! Why would someone make a comment *now*? Then, without warning, the tears came rolling down.

Before anyone could notice, I said I was going outside to get some air. I walked on the beach for a moment trying to digest this unexpected insult from a complete stranger. I just couldn't wrap my head around it. I had to leave. I told my uncle I had to go back to Vegas. I was on the road about an hour when it hit me: she hadn't known. She hadn't known I had just lost 140 pounds.

For some reason, I compared myself to a mentally retarded person. When someone is mentally retarded, you usually SEE (recognize) that and you excuse their behavior, *because* they are retarded. But what if, for some reason, they were retarded one day, but not the next? If they hadn't had time to get "smarter" yet, and someone saw them do something, well, retarded, they would call them stupid and maybe make fun of them, not knowing they were actually really retarded just the day before.

It dawned on me that maybe no one made any comments about me being fat before because I *was* fat. I was in a whole different category and wasn't worth making a judgment over because it was clear as daylight to any and all who looked—and most certainly should have been clear to me. This realization opened a whole new thought process for me.

When I was fat, I was confident and always happy; I *had* to be. I would walk into a room with total confidence and think, "Look at me; I am funny, smart, cute, etc... Quick, look past the fat and judge me for these other qualities, not for being a fat person." As I lost the weight, for some reason, I thought everyone would just *know* all these qualities I possessed when I walked into a room. After losing the weight, I wasn't as full of myself (no pun intended), I wasn't as confident, and I didn't do any positive self-talk like I did before, sometimes just to make it through the day.

I realized then that not only was I not fat anymore, but I also wasn't "special" anymore either. When I was heavy and went out, I would approach any guy I wanted. If he didn't want me, it *must be* because I was fat. NOW, why didn't he like me? I was taking things way too personally without my 140 pound crutch to lean on or to blame being rejected on. This was a huge mental wake up call.

Before, if there was a guy around who liked big girls—I was *it*. I was the cream of the crop (pun intended). I was the cutest fat girl around and I had no problem talking to, or meeting men. Now what was I? I was average. I was part of a much larger pool of prospects. I had to try *harder* to win people over and there was no way I could compete with those skinny bitches with blonde hair and fake ass boobs in short skirts and high heels.

It was even *harder* to sell myself with all my plastic surgery scars. I dated one guy who actually said in the heat of a drunken rage that I looked like a Raggedy Ann Doll with all my scars—and that my surgeon should be shot.

Having this second epiphany should have made a former 300 pound person feel *normal* and good, but it made me more depressed. As much as I didn't want to feel unique because I was fat, I quickly realized being average had a serious downside too. Many of my friends would say, "You look great, but I liked you before when you were fat; you were so much happier." In many ways I liked who I was, at least inside, better when I was fat too.

***

I actually was getting hit on a lot more by men now that I was smaller, but they weren't really men I was terribly interested in. I dated a guy who was emotionally bankrupt who would just call me once a month or so and spend a night or two with me and that's it. Can you even call that "dating"?

That's when I somehow found myself in love with not one, but two married men. They each had their unique circumstances, of course, or how else could I have justified my feelings for them, or the things we did? It would be easy to say, "Aren't there enough single guys out there?" It would also be true, but I do believe that you can't control who your heart goes pitter pat for either. That, and it takes two; at least for most things... Yes, yes, I know, but we *can* control our actions though! (Thanks, Doc, for reminding me!) For the most part, I was fairly respectful to both of the spouses, each in appropriately unique ways, and was *not* a "home wrecker." In fact, as far as I know *both* couples are still together to this day.

Anyway, it seemed the more men I had in my life, the more shallow and empty I felt. I felt like I was in one of those money whirlwind things, where you are surrounded by all this money, but you can't grab or hang on to a single Bill (Ted, Rick, Larry—you name him).

I decided to go worship the sun for a while. I loved running around the house naked and once in a while, I would step out in the back yard to put a rug out to dry. I loved the feeling of the sun and air on my body. That's what I wanted: something freeing—something that would put me back to a "special" zone, where all the facades we put up (or on) in life wouldn't be in the way.

That's how I found Common Ground in Las Vegas— where people just hung out naked!

My first time there I was greeted by a man named Stan who gave me a tour, explained the rules of conduct, and told me about all the characters I would probably meet as the day went on. Sure enough, all these characters showed up one by one and true to his word, they were just as he described; all wonderful people.

One guy Stan described as a typical big biker lookin' dude complete with long hair and a handlebar mustache was as kind and sweet as a giant teddy bear. There was a couple that were both school teachers, there was a supervisor for a local government agency, there were casino workers from bell hops to concierges, and there was even a police officer. There was a guy who wrote software, there was a woman who was a massage therapist (I guess she doesn't see enough naked people in her line of work). There was a couple that the wife was a nurse and the husband worked on secret government stuff (everyone knew this because of his distinct vague but standard 'no comment' answers when asked about his job. Being close to the Nevada Test Site it was not uncommon to know people who worked on secret stuff).

The cool part about being naked though, is you only knew what people did when they told you. You couldn't tell if they were a mechanic or an attorney; ya, they were there too. When you strip off the brand names (or not-so-brand names), you get to know the *real* person. It's almost ironic that while when someone is completely nude, you *can* see everything, but you work *harder* to make eye contact. Of course there are strict rules at nudist resorts that will get you tossed if you gawk, but it's almost refreshing to be forced, if you will, to make an eye-to-eye connection. You tend to listen more intently, as if you're seeing and feeling the words more than you're just hearing them.

My shaman nudist friend says this about being nude: "It is not impossible to lie when you're naked, but it's much easier to tell the truth." I guess this might be the idea behind the expression 'the naked truth'.

Some people played water volleyball, some bellied up (literally) to this cool tiki bar that Stan, the guy who gave me the initial tour, built. Some people just floated around the pool or worked on their all-over tans, and some played board games inside the club house where the air conditioner kept them comfortable.

I loved the nudist lifestyle. The freedom of the life-style and the new nudist friends I made became more important to me than dating. The feeling of the sun and air touching my body was like receiving gentle hugs from Mother Earth. The people in the nudist lifestyle are like no other; they love themselves inside and out, and see past the facade that clothes normally hide. They look in people's eyes and hearts. They appreciate each other as whole people, not just parts.

Funny—all I had to do was take off all my clothes to find them!

The Best Breaker-Upper

My brother had an "incident" that was finally enough to throw the book at him and send him to prison. I don't think there is any doubt that prison changes people—I think the real problem is it rarely changes people for the better. When my brother went to prison, the first time, he was in fact a changed man. He picked up the Bible, and wrote the sweetest and funniest, (but silliest) letters. To describe my brother is like trying to describe a villain folklore hero that you love to hate (or hate to love depending on the moment). He has a very unique charm (to everyone, not just women) about him that is undeniably and captivatingly cunning. He will give you the shirt off his back, but 10 minutes later, he will decide you really don't need those tires on your car, since you *now have* a nice shirt. Somehow he makes sense of it.

My brother is an amazingly talented, and sadly, very successful con-artist. I have never seen anyone con people out of things like he can. He will talk you out of the shoes you're wearing while he is telling you stories and making you laugh the whole time. You will somehow be *thrilled* to give him your only pair of shoes. You won't even realize he totally ripped you off until your feet are bleeding from walking barefoot for a day or two.

Just then, he will re-appear to "help you out." When you see him, you will start to yell at him for stealing your shoes, but he will look at you, smile, and tell you that it's all good because he has band-aides for you. They are the *only* ones in town and they are *only* $10 each. You won't mind buying his band-aides even though you probably have a cabinet full of them. Why? Because he promises he will use the money to go buy your Grandmother some flowers in the old folks home and visit her, since you can't, because your feet are bleeding.

He will remind you how much he is "helping *you* out." Somehow, you will think he is the greatest guy on the planet as he drives away in *your* car; after all, he is going to see *your* Grandmother, *for you*. He's such a great guy! You would think this is the last you would see of my brother, but nooooo, he will either con you out of more stuff, or make you look like an asshole for getting mad at him for the stuff he has already conned you out of. Yet, how could you possibly be mad at him, since he was on his way to see *your* Grandma when he ran into a guy that can get you the job/car/house/ whatever of your dreams and he has been *trying* to help *you* ever since he left... (with your shoes, car, and whatever else) you total ungrateful asshole, you.

But like the incredible hulk after he wakes up, when my brother went to prison (the first time) he metamorphosed into a really nice, funny, sweet (and actual apologetic) guy. After a while, I decided to go visit him and even brought a couple of his kids along. He was really changed! His oldest two kids took a while to come around because they had seen him in and out of jail so many times, and given him too many chances. They were just done. I told them, "You are probably right to feel that way; however, right now, he's a great guy so there is a window of time to see how he *can* be— so when he gets out, you can remind him that you *know* he *can* be *better*." They finally did come around and really enjoyed spending that time with him.

He was at a camp (minimum-security prison). It was so "minimum" that if the guys threw a ball over the fence, they would jump over it to get the ball and just jump back over. Seriously—the guards didn't mind because it saved them from walking a few feet, unlocking the gate, and retrieving it (of course, they justified their laziness as a "safety precaution" somehow).

There was a walking path around the outside of the fence. I asked my brother if the guards walked the perimeter sometimes. He laughed and said, "No, that's for us. They let us out to walk the perimeter for exercise. We all make fun of the guards because they are the ones in prison, not us. They have to sit in the 'bubble' by the radio, phone, and computer, and watch us from there; we can go outside and play all day." Of course, he *did* understand they got to go home to their families, too, but I can see how an inmate would look at this positive side of it.

Inmates at minimum camp often work for the Department of Forestry Service. They not only help fight fires when needed, but they do other community things like build shade structures at rest stops, shovel snow off pathways for elderly people in town, and of course pick up trash along the roads.

I was visiting my brother one day with his kids and there were tons of men just hanging around. I asked him, "What are all these guys doing here?" He laughed and said "Teresa, it's a male prison, duh!" He always had a way of making you laugh. Many of the men were saying, "Hi," because they all knew who I was through my brother talking about me. Of course, *I* didn't know *any* of them. He introduced me to a few as they walked by the outside of the fenced-in area we were in for visiting. "That's Styles," he said pointing to a hottie that he noticed caught my eye, "he used to be a hairdresser on the outside so he cuts our hair in here." "Hum," I said, "he's cute" in a nonchalant way, and said or thought nothing more about him.

A few days later, I got a letter from my brother and in it was another letter—from Styles. It was short, sweet, and to the point. He introduced himself and wrote that my brother apparently told him that I thought he was attractive (thanks bro, NOT). He let me know he thought I was very attractive too, and asked if I would like to be pen pals? His actual name was Tom Ross.

At the time, I was casually dating a guy who lived in California named Tom and I was also casually dating a guy in Vegas named Ross. I told him of this little coinkydink that his name was both of their names. Since I was dating both men casually, I said it would be no problem to just be pen pals. It only took about a month of letters before we knew we had chemistry and he confidently told me to dump both Tom and Ross and stick with him.

Yeah, I should dump two guys who have jobs, cars, etc. for a convict in prison—that makes total sense! Tom, lived a two-hour drive away in California, made $12 and hour digging ditches, was 10 years older than me, and rented a room in a friend's house. He had just gotten divorced after a 20-year marriage and lost everything; hey, it happens. The longer I knew him, I wondered more and more how much he really contributed to "their" property/assets anyway, but who am I to judge? However, he had no desire to do anything but dig ditches, and at his age, it was starting to wear on him hard. On one occasion, I talked about starting a very simple business with him and his face turned white with fear. That was pretty much the end of our dating.

My relationship with Ross was a little different. He had his own consulting business, his own house, and was doing pretty well for himself. He would call me on a Saturday morning and ask me what I was doing that night. Sometimes he would want to take me to a romantic dinner or to the drive-in with his kids, but once in a while, he would tell me he had a hot date and was wondering if I could babysit. I liked him a lot for his openness and honesty, and I adored his boys, so I was ok with this "relationship." I enjoyed time alone with him, with him and his kids, and also loved time alone with his boys; they were great—but I knew this wasn't going anywhere. So, yup, I dumped Tom and Ross for a convict in prison.

Teresa X. Roberts

While Tom was in prison, he never accepted a dime from me. He was very respectful in every way and he wrote the sweetest letters. I smiled all day at work knowing there was a love letter, almost every day, waiting for me at the Post Office. It was incredible how much joy that consistency brought me.

After one particularly stressful day at work, I wanted to just go straight home to kick off my shoes and soak in a bath, but I had to check my mail first. I opened my daily love letter and the handwriting was a little nicer than normal, and indented on each side centering it on the page. I thought, is he writing me a poem, a song, or what? He had written me a couple poems but they were short, and kinda dorky, yet adorable.

With a shake of my head, another day I'm in hell
I got out of bed, I wasn't feeling too well
I must go work for the day, some more work as a slave
I get pennies for pay, because I just can't behave
Then I saw her out there, I could see through the gate
The wind blowing her hair, it must have been fate
Fate decided to knock, and I opened the door
Honey, you really rock, and I'm screaming for more
I'm so glad that I wrote that very first letter
I don't mean to gloat, but it keeps getting better
At first it was scary, you were a mystery
But we started caring, the rest is history
We rise and we fall, we push and we pull
We give it our all, but we never get full
You gave me your heart, all your love and your care
Honey, we'll never part, and one soul we will share
There are so many ways I'm glad you're in my life
Marry me, Teresa, please be my wife.
All my love, Tom

Nope, this was no poem, it was a marriage proposal! My heart sank and jumped for joy at the same time, nearly flying out of my chest, as I read each word as slowly as he probably wrote them. It was the most romantic thing I have ever read.

***

I was the one who proposed to my first husband because I was tired of waiting for him to do it. We were standing in the kitchen of our crappy roach infested apartment in front of the ugly outdated refrigerator. We stopped to grab a quick hug in passing and I just asked him. Yeah, that *was* special, wasn't it? Not! But *this* letter? Oh Lord, this letter was like creamy velvety cream cheese frosting on top of a Godiva Chocolate Cheesecake with chocolate covered strawberries, and whip cream on top of that. Yeah, something like that! I said YES!

Tom was released on parole only about six months after we started writing; he did a total of about two years for trafficking. We agreed that when he got out, we would get married right away, before we had sex. It sounded good in our heads.

He was so respectful of my brother for setting him up with me, that he didn't want to step on his toes. Because my brother had planned to parole to my house, Tom decided to go to a half-way house until after my brother got out and got settled somewhere else on his own.

The Parole Officer let Tom come home with me for the weekend before reporting to the half-way house. We drove past the exit to the courthouse downtown and I said, "Are we going to do it (get married)?" He took a moment to answer and said, "No, let's wait." I was actually relieved! We went back to my place and had hot animal monkey sex. Yeah, that's right, I said that!

A couple weeks after he was out, we were having dinner at a Mexican restaurant. I was having a margarita and I offered him a sip. He said he could *never* drink. He mentioned that a lot and I wasn't sure at the time why he was so adamant about it. He had gotten a job as a waiter almost as soon as he got out. He was doing great and making about $100 a day in tips. He showered me with gifts and kept my car full of gas since I took him to work and picked him up when I could.

One day I got a call from his (girl) friend saying, "Tom is here, he is super drunk; he has to get back to the half-way house for curfew; you have to come get him." What? I thought he was at work. When I arrived, I was actually surprised to see he was falling over drunk. He got into the car as he was yelling at his friends, "Shee, I tole you she lovesss me, she'll do anythin for me becaussss she's bewtful and she lovessss me!"

I was so scared to take him back to the half-way house in this condition so I called the house manager and said he would be an hour late because he had to work overtime. He was in his work clothes, so this fib just might fly. He had one hour to sober up though I knew one short hour would not nearly be enough.

I got a call from him just 10 minutes after I dropped him off at the half-way house. "Teresa, please, I love you, please come get me." I turned around and as I pulled up I saw him, his bags, and the half-way house manager, on the curb. I got out and Tom practically said the same thing to the house manager that he had earlier said to his friends, but this time he *tried* to sound more sober when he said it.

I had a chat with the house manager while Tom waited in the car. He said Tom tried to say that he spilled beer on himself at work (which a waiter *could* do) and that's why he reeks of alcohol. The house manager admitted to me that he himself had a drinking problem for 30 years and for all of those years his wife tried to help him. It wasn't until the marriage ended that he realized he had to help himself. He tried to be brutally honest with me that Tom would never change for me either. He instructed me to take him directly to a rehab place immediately.

We pulled up to the rehab place and Tom wouldn't get out of the car. I tried to get the people inside to help me get him in there. They said he had to walk in *on his own*; yes, this did make sense but it also pissed me off! Tom finally got out of the car and said if I didn't take him home to *our* house, he was going to walk away. I said, "I am not taking you home." He said, "Teresa, it is a violation of my parole to drink. If I go in there for a drinking problem, I have to admit I have been drinking and then I go back to prison. I am not going back to prison," and then he walked away. I knew he was right. I also knew this wasn't going to get "fixed" by me taking him home—but I thought we could think about a better solution after sleeping on it, so I took him home.

The next month was filled with amazing blissful sex; flowers at least once a week for no reason, and great conversations snuggling together on the couch. He kept my car full of gas and he handed me all of his tip money every day to help pay my bills. However, about once a week, he would also go on a binge and do the stupidest shit.

He would call a bunch of party (girl) friends on his phone while he hid outside acting like he was going to check the mail or something. He picked fights with me just so he could storm out to call them and have them pick him up, only to come back the next day with flowers begging my forgiveness. He would grab my cell phone and look at the call history and then just drill me about people I called—but he wouldn't let me see *his* phone.

When I got the bill and saw how much he was talking to all these girls and put the time lines together, it was unbelievable. One time he claimed he was sleeping in the car for an hour when I couldn't find him, but the phone records showed he was talking to a girl in New York that whole time. I said, "Were you talking in your sleep to her, WTF?" He tried to say he had been "friends" with her forever and I shouldn't be upset. Well, A) if you've been friends with her forever, why am I just hearing about her now and B) with cell phones she could be across the street instead of New York for all I know.

He was amazing at making up though; I have to give him credit for that. I came home one day to find the following letter on my nightstand:

My Dearest Teresa,

I'm sitting here in your bed and I just realized I haven't wrote you a single letter since I've been out. What better time than now, while I'm laying here surrounded by your presence. I sit here and look through the letters I wrote and I look at the card on your dresser and I think to myself "There's not one word I've said to you that I didn't mean or wouldn't say again to you right now." I truly do wake up in the morning and count every day as another day I am thankful you came into my life. Thank you for today. Thank you for yesterday. And thank you in advance for tomorrow. I was wrong about our love being like Mt. Everest. Our love has not regressed, but has gone even higher to which there is no mountain on this earth to compare it to anymore. And I truly believe it will keep on growing. I am madly in love with you Teresa. And I am very excited to see what heights our love takes us to in the future. Until then, I am very satisfied with the pure bliss your love has me at now.

> *Your Husband,*
> *Tom*

That letter kept a roof over his head another week.

But the last straw was when he took my car to spend some time with his kids. I had a feeling something wasn't right so I had a friend drive me by his kids' place a couple times throughout the night; my car was never there. He came home the next morning, surprisingly sober, with all these stories of playing games with his son, how he fell asleep in his bed with him, and didn't wake up until this morning. He went on and on about how much fun he had, but now he was feeling frisky and wanted a quickie before he went to work. I had no idea what or *who* he had done that whole night, so needless to say, I was NOT feeling frisky at all. I calmly waited for him to get done with all his bullshit stories, blinked a few times, and said, "I went by your ex's house last night a few times; you were never there."

He went ballistic. Yelling, waving his arms in the air, "How dare you! How dare you check up on me and assume I am lying." I honestly don't know how I did it, but I just sat their totally quiet and watched him freak out while yelling at ME! "Now I suppose you're not going to give me a ride to work either and I will lose my job because you had to sneak around checking on me."

It was all I could do not to laugh hysterically out loud. To be honest, I hadn't even thought that far ahead. My thinking was more short term...like WE'RE DONE NOW! He stormed out to walk to the bus stop. I couldn't have him losing his job on "my" account of course (eye roll). I let him walk a bit, but then I picked him up and drove him to work. We did not speak the whole way and as I dropped him off, I calmly told him to come by later for his things.

When he showed up after work with one of his party (girl) friends, all of his things were neatly packed in plastic tubs and waiting for him on the covered porch.

He expressed his surprise and appreciation; "Teresa, I can't believe all my stuff is not thrown out in the streets in piles, you are the best breaker-upper I have ever been with." Wow. Now that is a trophy I should probably have—"The best breaker-upper award." I shall put it on my mantel to display to any future boyfriends to let them know they can walk all over me and I will be the best breaker-upper when it comes to "get the fuck out" time.

Love at First ~~Strike~~ Sight

I was on anti-depressants *and* popping Xanax like they were candy while Tom and I were together. A lot of our relationship *was* wonderful and I *did* love him very much. The sex was also amazing; the best I'd ever had.

He was never late to pick me up from work and was never short on romance (when he was home and sober). He was also a ticking time bomb that could explode at any time in an unpredictable drunken rage. I never knew if I was going to get Sober Tom or Drunk Tom. Toward the end, I learned he had gone back to smoking meth as well, which explained his calmness at times. They say if someone is normally hyper (as he was), then speed calms you down; whereas with a normal person, it speeds you up. He was normally high strung and bouncing off walls. However, he was calm when he did meth, which made it easy to notice when he was high.

So I found myself single again. Tom was the first real relationship since my 14-year marriage ended so it was tough. I knew without a doubt I could not be with Tom, mostly because I knew I could not help him. Quite frankly, I just didn't have the patience to compete with another addiction.

***

As I started to date again, I was super paranoid about men who said they were single; I always suspected they were actually married. I didn't want to go through that bullshit drama again. One of the married men I briefly dated before I met Tom, was Uriah. He was 11 years younger than me, incredibly yummy, and seemed to really appreciate me for me. He told me he was married from the start, but his wife was only with him for the insurance while they had their second child. Yeah right, I thought.

Well, after meeting his wife and the fact that she seemed pretty indifferent to him or my "friendship" *with* him, I accepted it as the truth. My first husband and I were practically just friends the last seven years of our marriage and even slept in separate rooms the last two years, so it seemed logical that he could be telling the truth. We dated for about 3-4 months, which included dinners, movies, cards and love notes back and forth, and of course lots of calls and texts. One day Uriah called me and said, "My wife wants to talk to you." "Okay," I said, not thinking anything of it. "About what?" "About us," Uriah said. "Us?—What about us?"

Still confused. Uriah took a deep breath, then let it out, and said, "She knows about us and wants to hear it from you."

My heart skipped a beat and my eyes started going dry from holding them open so long in complete cluelessness, but yet my mind was quickly catching up to reality. He went on to explain that he wasn't entirely honest with me but he loves me, wants to be with me (not her), and I can tell her anything and everything.... EXCEPT, that we had slept together. "WHAT?" I respond with. "Uh, where do I begin here... and if you want to be with me, not her, what difference does it make if we've slept together?" He indicated he was afraid she would not let him see the kids when they got a divorce. Hum....

I met her at a bar/restaurant, she slammed down two glasses of wine despite the fact that she was so pregnant she could barely fit in the booth. She was clearly nervous which I worked to my advantage. Rather than let her attack me, I asked her point blank, "Do you love Uriah?" She thought for a moment and answered "Yes." I said, "Then I don't matter, nor does anything that Uriah and I ever had together matter; what matters is that you go home and do everything you can to make your marriage work." She let out a huge sigh of relief and we just sat in silence for a minute or two. When we did resume talking, we counseled each other for two hours while Uriah sweated it out at home.

He expected (and wanted) her to come home furious, pack her bags and run to her Mother's house. Imagine his surprise when she came home with open arms asking him to make their marriage work. Uriah called me every horrible name including the C-word for "ruining" his "out" with her. Uh, you're welcome!

The other married man I met between my first husband and Tom was Vic. Vic was about four years younger than me and had the body of a God. We had instant chemistry and had many long conversations, though we never really went on a "date". My phone rang at work one day and it was his wife asking why my business card was in his wallet. I had asked Vic if he had a girlfriend, (since he wasn't wearing a wedding ring) and he answered, "No." Technically, he wasn't lying then, since he had a WIFE (eye roll).

Vic's wife was irate and went on and on about some *other* woman that he had an affair with for two years who was black (he was white) and that she had tattooed his name on her ass. Yes, she carried on with this drama that I could care less about, while I was at work. I told her he and I had nothing going on to which she disputed because *he* told her we did. I said, "Look, obviously he doesn't want to be with you, so why are you fighting to keep someone who clearly doesn't want the relationship?" She responded with, "I would leave him, but our dog is very old, and I'm afraid it would stress her out too much." Yes, she actually said this, I KID YOU NOT! I told her that was the lamest excuse for staying with a cheating asshole I had ever heard in my life, and hung up.

***

I missed Tom. Why? Why did I miss someone who lied to me, did who knows what with his stupid party (girl) friends, and verbally assaulted me when I confronted his lies. The sex was great, I mean REALLY great, but that's not what I really missed. I missed the romance parts. I missed the love letters that sparked our relationship before the fires of hell, fueled with alcohol, burned it down.

It took a bit of milling around in my head before I came to the conclusion that I didn't really need a man to be *here* for me, but it was ok if he was *there* for me. Briefly jumping back into the dating hell, er um, I mean *scene,* helped with this thought process a lot.

I went to a website that Tom had actually told me about when he was still in prison. I decided I would look for another pen pal. He would JUST be a pen pal. I would do this much "smarter" this time. I would have certain criteria: 1) He had to have a long time left to do; I didn't want him getting out and hurting me. 2) He had to be far away so I wouldn't be tempted to visit, even on a friends-only level. 3) Just to be sure, he couldn't be that good looking so I wouldn't fall for him. I didn't want to write to someone hideous either, mind you, but just not someone I would be attracted to and fall in love with.

Found him! He is doing LIFE; check. He is in Carson City, which is eight hours away; check. He's barely average looking; check. I proceeded to read his ad:

"I'm a great catch. I live in a big house with lots of windows, I have people who do my cooking and laundry so I don't have to, and I am an artist so you will probably get some cool drawings, and I even have a cat."

Okay, so he has a sense of humor. I had read other ads just for the fun of it, and there were always things that turned me off like using the "God card," meaning they are soooo good now that they have found the Lord; or else they went on and on about family being important to them (I would think if they were so important, you wouldn't be in there, right?); or the best ones of all, the "I'm looking for someone special in my life and I can parole to your house when I get out in two months." Eeeeks... I couldn't click off those ads fast enough.

One thing that is important to understand (that I would learn later all too well): men in prison are like puppies at the pound. They are so adorable and sad when they are locked up in those cages and they just wanna be loved, and held, and cuddled, and they will be *so* good and loyal if you just bring them home, feed them, give them a bath, and rub them just right, behind the ears—right?

But we all know the sad truth... A dog is often at the pound for the same reason a man is in prison... They are often damaged goods, or they are royally fucked up, and when you bring them home, you will know in less than 30 minutes which one it is. Then again, you might not learn until the first time you leave them alone and they get on your computer and infect it with viruses from porn sites, or just steal the damn computer and you never see them again. Er, uh, um, I mean, tear up your couch and shit on your carpet. Same thing, right? But at the time, I hadn't really learned this yet. Hey, I am a slow learner with a soft heart; not a good combo.

So I looked up his crime online; murder and kidnapping; 10-life on the murder charge with a 5-20 behind it for kidnapping. As odd as it sounds, I was less concerned with the murder than I was about the kidnapping. I think when most people hear "kidnapping" the first thing that they think of is "kid." For some reason, the first assumption that went into my head was a custody battle gone wrong and a "if I can't have our child, you won't either" scenario. Whoa, I was thinking way too deeply; stop, stop, stop. Be selfish here for a change. I just want a frickin' pen pal, that's all. I don't want to judge anyone, much less care that much about this person or what he did/didn't do.

I started the letter with something along the lines of "been there-done that" or "this isn't my first rodeo" or something clever I'm sure. I said that I fell in love with an inmate, he got out and was a POS (Piece of Shit) and I'm never doing that again, so don't get it in your head that this will EVER turn into anything more. I said I would write lots of letters because I love to write, I also travel to cool places so I will send tons of pictures, but indicated what I expect: "I expect at least one letter a week, if not more. If you can't do that, don't even write me back." In other words, I pretty much laid out my terms the best I could.

I got a letter about a week later saying all that sounds great, he didn't want a relationship either because it's just too hard and hurts too much when you have tons of time to do, and that he absolutely could write at least a letter a week, maybe more. Then he added, "But I am a little busy right now." WTF? I had to re-read that line a couple times before I continued on. He's *too busy* right now? I kept saying to myself.

When I finally read on, he explained that he was working to get ready for an art show that was open to the public in about a month. After that, he continued, he would shower my mailbox with tons of letters. Okay, maybe he didn't say that last part, but that was what "I" read.

Hum, art show? Open to the public? They let people like *you*, murderers and kidnappers, deal with the public? How does this art show work? Do you sit behind a chain link fence and does the public pass the money between the chain-linked fences with snipers closely watching from the rooftops? I had all these thoughts in my head; I was intrigued to say the least. I had been to many art shows, and I love them, but I had never been to one at a prison with murderers and kidnappers. This would be something interesting, not only to see, but defiantly someplace to buy something truly unique—or so I was thinking.

I had already planned a trip to Portland, Oregon, with my niece, nephew, and a girl I was sort of a nanny to. This trip was scheduled for a week after this art show. Xander and I had only written a few letters, which were nice, but meeting him was not the objective here; seeing this art show was something I just had to do. I bumped up my vacation plans a week since Carson City *was* on the way. The girl I was a nanny to had a sister that lived just south of Carson City, so we had already planned to stay there the first night of our trip anyway; stopping by the art show the next morning before heading up to Portland fit in perfectly.

We arrived at the Nevada State Prison; the oldest prison in the state. It looked like a castle or fortress of sorts. I really had no idea what to expect. I didn't want to tell Xander we were coming but I had to ask if kids could go to this thing. Knowing of my vacation plans, he replied, "Yes, kids can come, even nieces and nephews." Dang it. I was hoping I could just go in and if I saw him, fine, but I really didn't want to make contact per se.

One minor detail I hadn't thought about was the fact that the biological parents of the girl I was a nanny for, were in prison in another state. I hadn't considered how this might impact her hesitation of going into a prison. I learned of my oversight quickly when we got to the prison parking lot and she freaked and refused to go in; this presented a problem. I couldn't leave her in the car alone, or leave any, or all of the kids alone while I went in, especially in a prison parking lot; geez. So I thought, now what?

My niece, who was an amazing artist herself at the time and who also wanted to go in to check out the art, had her almost talked into going in. She finally said as long as I held her hand and didn't let go, she would go in. Ok—deal. We walked in and in about 3.5 seconds her and my niece were off running around checking out all the art, leaving me and my nephew in the dust.

We slowly walked around to all the vendors (inmates). They were sitting behind regular tables with their handmade crafts in front of them. They were all very pleasant and respectful. The girls caught up to me and my nephew by the time I had got to the last vendor. I recognized the art as Xander's but the man behind the table was not the same man in the picture he sent of himself; this guy behind the table was hot. It must be his cellmate or something; maybe he couldn't come out after all, I thought.

"So, are you heading up to Oregon?" He says. Ok, so Xander told the guy to look for a woman and three kids, I thought. I replied, "Ya." Then he said something, I forget what, but it was then that I *knew* it was Xander. I said, "Xander?" He said, "Ya." As my brain short-circuited and my thoughts went flying uncontrollably out of my mouth, "Holy fuck you're hot." I blurted out as I simultaneously watched my niece's jaw drop to the ground out of the corner of my eye. Not at what accidently came out of my mouth, but because she had pretty close to the same thought too. Oh, crap, crap, crap, crap!

I had never felt like that before. Never have I looked at someone and had my heart just about jump out of my chest like that. Never had I experienced "love at first sight" before. Until that moment, I thought "love at first sight" was a bunch of hogwash.

He was as cool as a tall glass of ice tea while we were chatting and I was visibly vibrating with nervousness once I learned it was him. As I walked toward the gate to leave, I kept looking back to wave, like a total lovesick dork. He was looking straight ahead paying no attention to me at all. What? Really? I thought. Finally, just as I got to the gate, I turned around one last time, and he gave a polite and extremely unexcited wave. For the next thirty minutes in the car, my niece practically chanted, "Teresa, he is HANDSOME. He is REALLY HANDSOME." Over and over. "I KNOW! I KNOW!" I said, with a "Damn it. Damn it. Damn it!" In my head.

The Power of the Written Word

On our trip, we went to all my favorite places in Portland, drove through part of the Columbia Gorge, had a blast winding down the Oregon Coast, and truly enjoyed a magical time driving through the Avenue of the Giants in Northern California. Yet, as much fun as I was having with the kids, in the back of my mind, I couldn't wait to get home to get Xander's letter about our first meeting anxiously awaiting to read what he thought of it.

All I could think about was how calm he had been. I kept pondering to myself, "Man, I can't even get a rise out of a guy who's been in prison for 11 years? Seriously?" Even though we had only written each other a short time, our letters had already become a *little* flirty.

So while the kids and I visited the Rose Test Garden in Portland, between snapping shots of them smelling roses, I kept thinking of the drawing of the rose Xander had sent me—it meant so much more all of a sudden. Xander had asked us to hug a tree for him in the Northern California Redwoods. I got the joke of course, because I had been there before, but the kids had no idea how difficult it would be to find a tree small enough to wrap our arms around. Still, I couldn't wait to get back home to send him the pictures of me trying to hug a tree for him.

I was just dying to come home and rip open that letter that I just *knew* would be waiting for me. I was also a little scared that maybe he wasn't interested in even being a pen-pal after meeting me—and all these butterflies in my guts were going to die a horrible death if that were the case. Sure—they'd make some butterfly collector a handsome catch—but I didn't want them dead and mounted, I wanted them alive! I had sent Xander a few post cards from the road but I tried my head off not to give up any hint about the butterfly activities going on in my belly. So, 'do the butterflies live or die?', was all I could think...

Finally, I made it home. The following letter, which I read, oh, about 14 times, was waiting for me when I got home:

Teresa X. Roberts

Dear Teresa,

"You don't know how bad I wanted a hug or kiss but I would have probably gotten shot. Handshakes are the only contact allowed out there. I'm still on cloud nine from meeting you. I could kick myself for being so shy. I felt like a little kid. I first saw you over by the woodcraft stuff—and to be honest, I didn't recognize you right off—you are so much prettier in person! You knocked my butt right off my feet. Nose over toes, even. And I only waited 'til Monday (Actually Sunday night) to write because I had to get a hold of myself. 'just pen-pals' is a whole new issue now" "Oh, and believe-you-me I'm not going to make it easy on you to keep things platonic. You've made it very hard. I have to admit I did see how pleasantly surprised you were which really got me charged up-and when you looked into my eyes... Oh my Gawd! I could actually feel heat in that look. That's never happened to me before."

-Xander

Yeah, the butterflies would live, but now they were acting like they were high on crack! Yes, there *was* something magical that happened when our eyes locked. By the end of August, not quite a month after meeting face-to-face, "we" were an "us," at least on some odd level. It was enough that we felt a discussion was in order regarding me continuing to date (or sleep with) people out here. He wrote:

"So 'we' are an 'us' now? Kinda slow ain't ya? Ha ha. I'd come to that conclusion a while back. Is that presumptuous of me? You're not sure what the boundaries are? I don't think that there need to be any boundaries. Unless you feel that you

need them. Does it upset me when you tell me about dates? Nope. But I will admit – I do feel a bit of jealousy. But I'm also realistic. You tell me--or don't tell me as you see fit. I DO NOT want you to ever lie to me. Not telling me about your dates isn't lying. Telling me you weren't dating when you were, would be. I won't ask you to stop dating and I don't really expect you to. That would be your decision to make-- not mine. You're a strong, smart, independent woman, you don't need a man, especially one in prison, trying to tell you what to do."

A few letters later, he informed me of his philosophy about love:

"Love, my dear, is no illusion. A concept, a chemical reaction, an ideal—sure—but much more. It's a total giving over of one's self to another. It goes beyond trust—to 'it just is.' A physical, tangible sharing of your soul with another. It may not last forever—nothing does. At least not all of it. But a part of it does go on forever. Love is not just an emotion—it's a spiritual experience—and the power behind all creation. And it's a release of all doubts and speculations, it's hard to do—and easy to do. Sure you may get hurt. Fuck it. You can break a tooth eating a Hershey bar—but chocolate is good! It all boils down to fear and getting past your own ego. And by ego I mean much more than just how you see yourself—or what others think about you."

I honestly didn't think of Xander as *another inmate* at all. Well, of course, the reality of it crossed my mind. Do I want to do *this* again? Do *what* again? I thought. Tom was a man. He had a drug problem, honestly no different than Rob had a gambling problem, or I had an over-eating problem. Xander didn't have an 'addiction' problem. He wasn't even a career criminal; he made one bad choice. Granted, it was a fairly LARGE bad choice, but he was definitely not in the same class as Tom other than they both had a penis.

***

Xander started to call by that fall and we were engaged before Christmas of that same year. No, you didn't miss it, we still had not had a live visit other than our brief first meeting, and we had not even shared a hug or a kiss yet. Letters, my friend, are the shit!

Yes, I had seen Tom in person, and had seen Xander in person, and was very attracted physically to both men; however, the written word is extremely powerful. Sometimes it can be read differently by the reader than the writer intended, but sometimes there is no mistaking the meanings, thoughts, and feelings behind the words.

Of course, when writing, you can take your time; articulate, concentrate, think, strategize, and fantasize with each tasty, tempting, tantalizing word. You can be someone, anyone, whoever you wish to be. You can make a reader happy, sad, angry, torn, confused, in love or thoroughly pissed off with key words, phrases and handy dandy **BOLDING**, underlining and my favorite, "quoting," used best, in my opinion, when trying to express sarcasm.

Forgive the irony, or pun, whichever it is, but words cannot express how powerful a hand-written love letter is. This is especially true with letters from someone in prison where words on paper are like little song birds they can release from the prison walls and be sent directly to your heart. Those little words, full of crap or not, can have a huge effect, especially when your day was filled with backstabbing office politics bullshit all day.

***

While I was at work I would have fantasies of throwing a few co-workers into a pile of cow manure and then giggling and pointing at them when their cute little suit and hairdo weren't so *perfect* now. Or sometimes I would imagine tearing their oh-so-ridiculous presentation material about their unrealistic goals for this quarter, into shreds. In my mind, I would throw the newly made confetti in the air while laughing hysterically. Though I am sure I am not the *only* office worker who had (or has) these reoccurring daydreams, it just didn't seem ridiculous to me to also fantasize about true love with an incarcerated murderer. When I'd get poems like the following from him, my whole world would suddenly seem illumined by a light greater than the sun:

Teresa X. Roberts

Someday

Teresa my love, when the waiting is done
We'll saddle our spirits and fly.
We'll sail past the seasons and circle the sun,
And skim the dim reaches of sky.
We'll rein our bright souls to some cosmic spire
Embrace on wild planets flung far.
Lie our communion in warm stellar fire
And purchase our own private star.
Our love never ending and high as the moon
At fevered pitch and thundering on.
Race with me through the time, morning and noon
We'll be first to reach the dawn.
Shrieking past heaven 'til the Summerland calls
Rising and falling together as one.
Our love will live as night surely falls
Sailing on and on when waiting is done.

I love you.

His poetry inspired me to return the favor in kind; however, mine was less fluid and much dorkier:

Why I Married A Murderer

When my heart found its home
You were meant to be a pen pal - that was all
Not a short order though - actually its rather tall.

They say I expect too much from friends
But if they can't deliver, that's where it ends.

You were a great correspondent from the start
It didn't hurt at all that you soon sent some art.

I chose you because you were average looking
Little did I know what fate had cooking.

I went on vacation and stopped in for a visit
I couldn't believe my eyes - that isn't you, is it?

At first sight, you knocked me off my feet
I felt it clearly – my heart skipped a beat.

I knew when I saw you our pen pal days were through.
I knew in my heart that I wanted something new.

We spoke for a bit – all too brief
The thoughts in my head were beyond belief.

From that moment on, it's been all new
For the reasons I chose you – I had only two.

I chose you because you were serving life
I never dreamed I would long to be your wife.

Thoughts of you brighten every minute of every day
Drawn together - now with time, we both must pay.

For many years a true love we both have sought
Now we count the days till we can tie the knot.

A cheesy poem by Teresa

113

Oh yes, the written word is powerful—powerful enough to get lost in—which is exactly what I needed at the time. I had just lost over half my body weight. I had become the person that I always *thought I was* inside, but yet, when it came out, I didn't recognize her anymore. I didn't need to behave a certain way to win people over anymore; not that I ever *did* need to, but it became a part of who I was for so long that when the weight was gone, somehow my confidence melted away with it. I needed a new identity. I needed a new purpose.

Paper Proposal

My Angel Afar,

My heart rages in my chest at the mere thought of you. That oh so briefest of touches we shared so long ago has left me filled with desire. A friendship turned to love with a simple gaze into your eyes.

Time and distance have taken leave of reality and foundation. So far away, you are. At the same time two have become closer than one in my soul. It is clear to me that there is no more to this world than reason can explain. Magic and the divine have brought us together to fulfill a need for something, anything in this world to be right. And in its perverse way, to keep what is right at a distance. A distance that can't last and won't be allowed to go on forever.

My soul has been brushed by the wings of an angel. Never again will I be whole without you. The waiting is done. My love for you will not allow me the convenience of delay. The beauty of your spirit is a shining light in my darkness. A beacon to guide me to hope. The depths of your heart and mind draw me in as your beauty draws forth my desire.

I am a man not worthy of the precious gift that is your love. And a man that will not relinquish that gift. That gift is a gift I return 10 fold with all of my love and all of my soul. I promise to devote myself to you above all others and to love you all of my life. To support and believe in you in all things. To share my life and all of its aspects with you. To stand between you and all danger. To swear my oath of life and love to you.

My sacrifices before yours, my blood before yours, my honor before yours, my life before yours. All of these will I give freely to protect yours. All I have and all I am is yours if you will reach out and accept what I offer. And in return I ask only the same of you. No trivial request, but neither is the offer. I offer all I have to give. All that is precious and has value in my life I give to you freely, and yet not so. This I understand for although it is offered freely—to be accepted it must be returned in kind, for this is the nature of such oaths. And has always been since the beginning.

I have searched my heart and know its depths; and in those depths I find your shining face. Take the time to know your heart-search deeply-and if you find me within—then let nothing of this world or any other keep us one from another. Join with me—heart to heart, soul to soul; as companion, partner, consort and bride. Be my wife as I, your husband. Let us walk this spiral path of life together, knowing never again loneliness. Knowing that one another is forever loved and cherished, desired and supported, trusted and valued, depended upon and needed. Let us live for each other and for ourselves in doing so. Let us be who we are, and be better for having each other.

Thus the first step was taken with paper and ink, it is only fitting this most important step be also taken in kind. Life is life and fear is its foe. Be with me. Love me. Join me in this life. I love you. I want to be with you and my greatest desire is to join with you in life.

I am yours. Heart and Soul. All you need do is reach out and embrace our love with me. Life is life. Fickle and unpredictable. Full of joy and tragedy. A promise of perfection is a falsehood. Perfection is not possible at this time and place. But the highs and lows are what give life its wonder and zest. Together with the understanding and support life can be so much more. I'm not asking or expecting perfection nor am I offering it. No lies or illusions. Only the reality of love and commitment. A partnership for life. And so much more.

I love you like no other. Join with me hand to hand – heart to heart, hand fasted and heart joined. Be my wife and take me as your husband. Marry me Teresa. I will love you all my life.

With all the love I have to give,

Xander

First Kiss

After waiting four long months, my visiting application was finally approved. I drove up to Carson City (400 miles north of Las Vegas) with another woman I had met at a Friends and Family of Incarcerated Persons (FFIP) meeting; she was going to visit one of her two sons that were in prison. It was the weekend before Valentine's Day. Nervous, awkward, scared, excited, anxious, are all simple words on paper. They do nothing to really express how my stomach and heart were feeling as I sat in the visiting area waiting for my future husband, a convicted murderer (how's that for a Valentine?), to walk in. Since we were engaged, even if it was only through letters, it was only natural that we would take this opportunity to kiss on our first embrace (you are allowed 10 seconds to hug and kiss on greeting and parting during visits). The anticipation was surreal to say the least.

And of course I had the usual thoughts that anybody in my situation would have (right?—now all you ladies who've gotten engaged to a convicted murderer after just seeing him one time for 10 minutes and then falling in love through letters, raise your hand and tell me if you didn't have these same exact thoughts): What if he is a terrible kisser? What if I am not attracted to him after all? What if he is not attracted to me? What if he makes a funny noise with his nasal cavity and sounds like a Sleestak when he talks? What if he thought *I* did something weird or annoying? What if we simply just didn't get along face-to-face?

Would this be a torturous six-hour visit that felt like a life sentence or would it go by in the blink of an eye? Would we really show our true selves? Is there really time for that? Does anyone even *do* that on a first 'date'? How can you even *be* your true self sitting at a table facing the watchful eyes of two scary looking guards just waiting to catch you doing something against rules (that I would later learn could change on a whim)?

Is the vending machine food any good and will I even be able to eat it with my stomach jumping around like it is? Are the other inmates that will be coming in for visiting going to be ogling me? Are they going to tell Xander that I'm hideous and he could do better just because they are jealous their mothers are the only one's still coming to see them?

So yeah—a million questions flying through my head at a mile a minute! It was like I'd never been in love before!

Well—had I? I had to wonder. This felt so different. You know, different because everyone else I had fallen in love with prior to him didn't have a life sentence and our first dates didn't involve metal detectors, dress codes, and the possibility of full body cavity search.

The moment of truth was fast approaching. When he entered the room, my heart nearly popped out of my chest. Lord! He was even more handsome, if that was possible, than the day we met! His eyes locked with mine as they did that first day—but only for a millisecond. I grabbed hold of him like I was in a burning building and he was the fireman coming to rescue me—yeah, it was tight!

And then the kiss. OMG he is an ahhhhhhhhsome kisssssssserr.... Oh, oh, oh, my knees, my knees... Please don't give out on me now. Holy crap! Yes, I was going to marry this man! Pinch me now to make sure this isn't a dream!

We sat at a table in the manner we were instructed to do so by the guards. He was shaking like crazy. You would think this would have me worried that he was scared, but it actually put me at ease and made me less nervous; he had enough nervousness going on for both of us, so I was okay. He was smiling from ear to ear which confirmed I wasn't that hard to look at, and his face showed no signs of regret or a desire to run for the hills (he would have been shot if he tried anyway).

That visit lasted six hours—but I was able to come back the next two days also. So the first day was great, I reflected blissfully as I lay in the hotel bed that night. But darn if my old mind wasn't racing again: Would we run out of stuff to say by the third day? Crap, we had covered so much in letters and phone calls! What if it was all over—nothing more to say! What if boredom was waiting just around the corner, as it always seemed to be! Hell, I swear we had communicated more before we even kissed than most couples do their entire marriages. Aaaaand that first visit did fly by...I don't even remember if we got up to pee! I know we ate though because I remember neither of us wanted to stop holding hands long enough to pick up our food. Somehow we managed.

Others around us had been playing cards and games—and I remember wondering: Did *he* want to play card games? Our visit was beyond exciting for me, but I was his first visitor in years so I know it meant a lot to him to be able to enjoy that time to the fullest, so I wanted to do whatever *he* wanted to. I asked him the next day if he wanted to play cards. He looked at me with absolute fear in his eyes and he said, "No! That would mean letting go of your hand and I *don't ever* want to do that." I was elated over his perfect answer!

Somehow we spent 18 hours over three days holding hands every second we could—and never ever even coming close to running out of things to talk about.

On the third day, Sunday at 2:20, one of the guards stood up from the table in the front of the room (where his beady little eyes kept a close watch on us *in particular* it seemed) and bellowed, "Visiting is CLOSED!"

Ah—those words—putting an end to our three days of enchantment. But it wasn't as sad as I thought it would be—though it was pretty sad. I think I was still too excited to be sad. We were still in love with writing and phone calls, so I imagined that we were probably both anxious to put our thoughts down on paper as soon as we could. I was on cloud nine the whole eight-hour drive home.

I practically jumped up and down like a first grader playing hopscotch when I got home to find my letter waiting from Xander. I couldn't wait to read it!

I knew that he would have known that I visited that weekend. He would have known that this would be the first letter that I came home to. I *knew* it would be something about the anticipation of our visit, something like: "I hope it went as well for you as I know it did for me!" So many thoughts running through the smile tattooed in big prison block letters on my heart.

First Fight

I got home—and sure enough, there it was. It read:

Dear T.

Hi Shmoogly. How're you?
Thank you for the nice cards and photos. You're so pretty. I
love them and I love you! I really do.

But I'm also very mad at you right now. Your little story
about trust and humiliation leading into your statement about
wanting to ask my Step-Dad about my ex and 'why or how he
confirmed it.' And your hints about how I should "admit any
falsehood" is way too much. Too far and too insulting. I told
you before that I've had about enuff of you checking up on eve-
rything I tell you. Well I'm DONE with that shit. I'm not

123

Tom and I'm done being treated like I am. I don't give a shit what Tom or Ross or any other dude did to you. I'm not them. You need to get over your trust issues. DO NOT marry me if you don't trust me. Period. I trust you-completely-and I expect that in return.

You shouldn't be worrying about if "anything he says will change things between you and me forever." Right now you should be worrying if something YOU say or do will. And let's just make it a little harder for you-shall we. MAYBE I lied. MAYBE I didn't. I DO NOT want you to even discuss the issue with my Step-Dad. You either accept what I've told you or you don't and we'll take it from there. And I'm going to call my Step-Dad and ask him not to discuss it with you-and to tell me if you ask. I'm done having you run around checking up on me. And I've decided that I'm not opening my friends here up to that either. And it doesn't matter anyway-NONE of them agreed to it. The basic consensus was "Jr. High is over." "Grow up" and "tell her that if she wants to know you, to talk to you, not everyone else."

I DO understand "what you are trying to say" all too well. You are saying that you don't believe me or trust me. Well-guess what-I'm not a little kid-I don't need you checking up on me. You need to decide if you want to trust me and be with me or play detective. It won't be both. The entire issue of my ex and what happened is closed. I told you what went down-and either you believe it or not. There are already WAY too many people involved in OUR life. With way too much influence over how you think and act. This is OUR relationship. You tell me something and I believe you. Period. No other considerations. I don't write your sister or ask your friends to confirm what you say. Do not do that to me. All it shows me is that you have very little respect for me, and for 'us.'

124

You tell me what you want to tell me or tell me want you want me to know. Period. I'll do the same with you. And that's all that should matter. If you don't see the problem with what you are doing – and why it pisses me off.... I don't know what to tell you. You are so worried about "what-ifs" that you miss the "what-is".

See-one bad thing and you focus on it-and forget about the rest. Teresa-you have got to see how wrong this crap is. Or is this just a way for you to push me away? If it is-it's working. And this last one is the last straw for me. Way too far, girl. So you need to step back and take a long look at how you feel and what you want. And you need to come to terms with these trust issues you have. I'm done paying for what other dudes did to you. I'm asking you to make a choice. Either let it go-or hold on to your distrust and it'll eventually ruin "us". Its your hang up so it's your choice. But I'm not going to have you bring my Step-Dad or anyone else into this. Either you respect and believe me or you don't. I love you, and I want you to be my wife. But without respect and trust, we can't get married. I love you! I love you! I love you! [he signed his name to end the letter, but scribbled it out to continue chewing my ass some more] But I am fucking pissed. You couldn't have insulted me more if you tried, not to mention how silly and embarrassing it'd be for both you and me to go and ask my Step-Dad some shit like that. I'm sure he'll be very impressed with you for running to him to check up on me. Oh my gawd woman! What is wrong with you?

So-in case I wasn't clear in all this rambling- I DO NOT want you calling my Step-Dad or asking him about anything. Or anyone else. I want you to figure out how you feel-what you think and what you're going to do on your own. I'm

NOT going to reassure you either. Maybe it's all a lie, maybe it's not. You decide and then decide what you're going to do. And how this affects our future.

I love you, sweetheart! But right now I want to tie your eyebrows in a knot. I love you. I hope you can get past this hang up of yours and make the right decision. And I hope you respect me enuff to stop questioning everything.

I love you.
Xander

THUNK.

A little background so the letter makes sense (*if* that is possible): Xander had told me that his ex-fiancé and his daughter had died in a car accident. He learned this, he said, because her new boyfriend had returned a letter, unopened, that Xander had written her, with the words, "Sorry, they died in a car accident," written on the back of the envelope. Xander said he asked his Step-Dad to confirm their death and that he *had* in fact regretfully confirmed their death. I bought his story; why wouldn't I? However, shortly after Xander and I got serious, through letters and phone calls, he said his ex-fiancé contacted him out of the blue telling him she was remarried and that her new husband wanted to adopt his 16-year-old daughter.

He claimed this was the first he had heard from her since he thought they were dead, and he was puzzled himself why she mentioned nothing about him not writing them in all this time. There were a few questions in my mind and they really *didn't* point to him "lying" but something did seem fishy. I was way more curious why his Step-Dad would lie to Xander—which is why I told Xander I was going to ask him about it; I honestly thought Xander would be *just as* curious, *if not more so*, to the point of being furious, as to why his Step-Dad lied about their deaths.

The reference to me talking to his friends stemmed from me asking if I could write to his friends, since he had not only begun writing to *my* friends and family, but a handful had gone through the painful application process and trekked the eight hour drive each way just to meet him, not to mention the family members (his and mine) that I flew from three different states to meet and visit with him. I thought we were starting a life together and to me, that means getting to know each other's families and circles of friends. I didn't think it was asking too much at all to introduce myself to his friends, as he did mine.

When I read his letter, not a single word really sunk in. ALL OF THEM DID – ALL AT ONCE. He knew I would come home to this? After our very first visit? After our very first embrace? After our very first kiss? We had 18 blissful and totally utopia filled hours gazing into each other's eyes—and he knew I would come home to *this*? And said NOTHING? What the Mother Fuck?!

I was sitting on the edge of my bed, numb, holding these words in my hand that felt like 60 grit sandpaper raked across my heart. No, what am I thinking? It didn't feel like sandpaper, it felt like Jaws had just taken a bite out of my heart and soul. All I kept thinking was "ask me anything—I'm an open book; you can even look up all my info in public records if you want—I have nothing to hide," which he had written in letters months earlier, and reminded me of *repeatedly*.

I thought, what the hell is he that upset about if he is NOT lying? But mostly I thought, He *knew* I would come home to this after that amazing visit? This was *definitely* our first fight! Game on! This is total bullshit... How DARE he talk to me like this after I gave him my heart and said yes to his marriage proposal. How DARE he talk to me like that after all I am giving up for him as it is. Just then the phone rang—it was him.

HA—he was sweet as pie! He started with his usual, "Hi honey," and started telling me how amazing our first visit was. My mouth started to feel like Death Valley, wide-open and drying out quickly. Is he serious? Is he mental? How could he not remember writing this horribly vicious letter? I finally brought my lips back together; let my mouth salivate for a moment with venom of my own, while I waited for him to take a breath. Then I let loose: "ARE YOU FUCKING SERIOUS?" "Uh, excuse me?" He replied in a super snotty tone, another world from the lovey dovey "our first visit was amazing" he just had a second ago.

I repeated, "Are you fucking serious? You KNEW I would come home to this letter and you said NOTHING during our '*amazing* first visit'? You sat there, looked into my eyes with nothing but pure love, and the whole time you KNEW I would come home to this? You didn't have the BALLS to discuss this in person? This issue, that is apparently sooo f'n serious to you that you ripped my head off for three and half pages? What the hell? Who the fuck do you think you are talking to me like this?!"

I had NEVER even raised my voice to him before this so screaming was a big deal for me at the time. I was done with my verbal assault. I was a little nervous because he did have a point (if he really wasn't lying), but he went way overboard and he spent entirely too much effort slamming me for doubting him that it pretty much confirmed he *was* hiding something, and probably something much bigger than I had scratched the surface on.

I was quietly waiting and getting prepared for his retaliation of my verbal assault. This would be our first fight; how was it going to play out? Would this be the end? One visit and one fight and we are done? He gently and softly spoke:

"Honey, when I walked in that visiting room that first day and our eyes locked, I couldn't remember my name. You were so beautiful you took my breath away. My heart was beating a million miles an hour just being next to you. At the end of our visit the first day, I couldn't even remember a single thing we talked about, I was still so taken back by what an angel you are. Even at the end of the third day, I came back to my cell and I went to change shoes and I swear, I couldn't remember how to even tie my shoes; how in the world could I possibly remember I sent that letter a few days before our visit?"

Our first fight, and the subject and content of the letter were dead. That fast.

The REAL letter I was waiting for that captured our visit came the next day and was just a *little* nicer than the ass-chewing one:

Dear T.

Hi Wife! I love you SO much! Do you know that? My brain is still all scattered from our visit. I just can't put into words how great it was to be able to see you and touch you and look into your eyes! I feel like I'm high. I've REALLY never felt like this before!

I hope you had a quick and safe trip home. I have to go-I just can't think straight. I just want to lay down and re-live every moment with you. I'll write more tomorrow. I love you.

Hi Baby! It's Sunday night at 6:00pm and my shirt really smells like you & your perfume. I love that! And I love you! So, now that we've had our visit – and you've had a couple of days to think about it, how do you feel? Do you still want to marry me? I sure hope so-because I want to marry you more than ever. I love you. You make me SO happy! I hope that I can make you just as happy. And I really hope I can get trans-ferred down there soon.. If they give me too much grief about it – I may need to ask you and my Step-Dad to make a couple calls to help it along – but we'll see. I just want to be closer to you! So we'll see.

> *Your Husband,*
> *Xander*

Not the Average Wedding Drama

A very good friend threw the most fun and interesting bridal shower. Everyone was instructed to wear blue jeans and a blue denim shirt (typical inmate attire). At the door, she attached a TBP (Teresa's Bridal Party) number to guest's shirts to mimic an inmate number. She then gave guests their choice of plastic handcuffs or a harmonica. We played some games and I got some pretty unique gifts. One of my favorite was a cake mix box with a nail file taped to it. Attached to the box was a note that read, "You know what to do."

When you marry an inmate, there isn't a whole lot of planning or prep work to do for the "big day," but there are a few tasks that are a little different than normal. Getting the warden's written permission to marry an inmate is required to get a marriage license (since the inmate can't be there in person, obviously). Having the prison chaplain call me to do an "interview" over the phone to make sure I was aware of his crime, how much time he had left to do, and to inform me of the higher than usual divorce statistics—was a little out of the ordinary.

I had met the chaplain once while visiting Xander so at least I had a face to go with the name. The chaplain was Christian of course, which made it very surprising when he said, "Teresa, I have to be honest with you. Sometimes I don't like my job. My door is always open for inmates in need of someone to talk to and I am the one who must deliver bad and unfortunate news more often than I would like. I work with a lot of inmates and 95% of them, I honestly would rather not deal with sometimes. Xander is not one of them. Even though Xander and I differ on our religious views, I like him and enjoy talking with him very much; he is in the top 5% in my book."

The fact that Xander was Wiccan, made his opinion even more impressive and reassuring to hear. I would say it took a huge weight off my chest, but it really didn't. I already knew in my heart the chaplain was telling the truth. Xander was a charmer and had a way with people; he was very knowledgeable, friendly, and likable. He was not your typical thug career criminal—not by any means.

While I was handling the few arrangements out here in preparation for our *glamorous* (not) wedding ceremony in the visiting room, Xander had some serious stress to deal with inside. He had a job in the prison book-bindery and since he was an artist, one of his jobs was designing. As he told the story, his boss was looking for a design to put on t-shirts to represent custom motorcycles built by inmates. A year previous, he had submitted a design as an entry in a contest to choose a logo. They chose another logo instead of his so he sold his drawing at the prison art show where we first met. It should be noted that all inmate art had to be "approved for sale" *prior* to the art show.

His boss saw a copy of this drawing and said, "That's what I want." Xander politely told her he would be happy to draw something *like* that, but she couldn't use *that* drawing because he sold the original and now that person "owns" it. She informed him she would not pay him to draw something *like* that when she could just have *this* drawing that was already done. Xander made the grave decision to delete the electronic file so she couldn't have it. Oh boy! He was immediately given three disciplinary write-ups and sent to the hole just a few weeks before our wedding date.

One write-up was for disobeying orders, another was for destroying prison property, but the third...the third was the best of all: Copyright Infringement. WTF? The drawing was his, he drew it in his cell, and SHE demanded it. She claimed that because he worked in the bookbindery, ANY AND ALL drawings of his, done while working or in his cell were property of the bookbindery and since he sold *their* property at the art show, he violated Copyright Infringement laws.

The prison actually had an official form that stated the bookbindery owned any art work an inmate employee drew; however, Xander had never seen this form, much less signed one. They forced him to sign one after they sent him to the hole, and of course rather than dating it when he started working in the bindery like they wanted him to, he dated it AFTER the date of the write-ups which was his second rebellious, yet legally rightful, jab.

The prison assigned an Internal Investigator to this matter. They wanted to press additional charges to the tune of 5-20 more years, and a possible $100,000 fine, or something ridiculous like that. Because Xander had sent me a lot of art, guess who *else* was being investigated? Yup, yours truly. I was threatened with criminal charges including Copyright Infringement, in addition to possession of stolen property.

It was about a month and a half of stressful hell. I saw an attorney who was almost salivating to get the case because the prison was clearly in the wrong; however, he couldn't talk his partners into doing it on contingency. Meanwhile, Xander sat in the hole for about six weeks as I prepared for our wedding and did my best to dodge going to prison myself over some total bullshit. The allegations (or I should say 'threats') were eventually dropped, as well as two of the three disciplinary write-ups he received.

Talk about justice! If you ask me, the real criminals are *running* the Criminal Justice System.

***

Well, since convention was the last thing on my mind, I decided to take my honeymoon *before* the wedding. Hey, why should there be anything normal about my wedding, or me for that matter? I went with a friend on a camping trip where we planned on visiting a few nudist/naturist resorts before swinging around to Carson City for the wedding. I wanted to go on this trip alone, but my mother-hen friend talked me into taking this weirdo friend of ours—"for my safety." He drove me insane the whole trip.

First off, this guy was one of the thriftiest people I have ever met in my life; he would obsess about getting the best gas prices to the point of having me drive 10 blocks out of my way to make sure I was saving a penny a gallon. At the time of our trip, 7-11's were offering 49cent re-fills when you brought in your own cup. This guy went out and bought a gallon jug-sized mug and demanded he be allowed to fill it for 49cents every time we stopped. And yes, he would actually drink that much Diet Coke, which meant we had to stop to pee. A LOT!

We arrived in Carson City and I got my usual room at the Motel 6 that I had stayed at so many times before when I came up to visit. My weirdo friend had given up on trying to talk me out of marrying Xander so I got ready that morning in total silence. Visitors, even brides-to-be, have dress codes to follow when entering a prison facility. Visitors are not allowed to wear any blue, white, or orange (as if anyone would want to wear orange anyway). There are other rules for attire and accessories, of course, but the reason those colors are not allowed is because they are possible colors the inmates wear and if there was a sudden mad dash for the gate, they want to know who to shoot. Because I couldn't wear white, I had a pagan type black and red dress custom made which I thought Xander would like. The dress was awesome and I was beautiful in it.

Because Xander was in the hole, he was only allowed a two-hour visit instead of the normal six-hour visit. It was also on a specific weekday instead of the weekend. The advantage to a weekday visit was that the visiting room wouldn't be full of screaming kids, or their parents gawking at us during our vows, with the vending machines as our backdrop. The downside was that we got the scariest and creepiest of the bunch. This "special" visiting day was only for those who were in isolated segregation—usually for good reason—or in protective custody—usually for reasons you would rather *not* know. Xander did not fit in even with the *regular* inmate crowd, much less these Charlie Manson looking ones!

Xander and I sat across from each other at the table (another *special* rule for these 'special' inmates). We held hands, gazing into each other's eyes, nervous, excited, a little giddy, while we waited for the pastor to arrive. We waited, and we waited, and we waited. We tried so hard not to keep looking at the clock ticking our two hours away, minute by minute. Where was he? It's not like you can whip out your cell phone and call him or even run out to the car. Once you leave visiting, that's it, you're done.

After we waited over an hour or so, the guard who actually knew us well by then, made a few phone calls unbeknownst to us. He approached our table and said, "Sorry, I guess he went to the other prison next door and they told him there was no wedding scheduled for today so he left... he's not coming back."

I do believe the guard honestly felt bad for us but there was nothing anyone could have done, rules are rules. Looking back, you would think the pastor not showing up should have been a huge sign.

I called him immediately after I left visiting, right from the prison parking lot. I left the nastiest message— that I drove 400 miles to come up here and now I have to reschedule and drive all the way back. He didn't need to know I went on a nudist resort vacation and circled around on my way home to get hitched, right? The fact remained, I was not a married woman and I had to re-schedule and drive back again to be one.

At least he was out of the hole by the time we could reschedule so we could have our six-hour visits for three days, which *was* nice. I bought another dress because, of course, the beautiful one I had custom made, now had bad luck. When you marry a murderer in prison, you need all the luck you can get after all.

We wrote our own vows but due to the complete anal-ness of "procedure" and that you don't dare ask for anything special when you're in prison, we went with whatever the pastor normally did. It wasn't that horri-ble actually. We exchanged our vows through letters and read them to each other over the phone prior to the *lovely* ceremony in the prison visiting room.

Another oddity that should have been a sign was that rather than the spectacle they usually force marry-ing couple to put on by exchanging your vows in front of the vending machines, was that they let us go into a side room with windows. Initially I thought it was nice to have a little privacy—until the pastor had us stand right in front of the mural on the wall. It was an ocean scene with huge fish and out of the corner of my eye was a shark that looked like it was going to eat me whole. Well, so much for signs.

Our Vows

Mine

You once told me that the left side of your body represented the dark side of your life.

So in said regard, it might seem unfitting for you to wear this symbol of my love on your dark side.

However, I have given this a lot of thought... I ask you now, to let this ring close the door on your dark side and serve as a reminder that our love is the birth of a new life.

Xander, I give you my love... during the fun and not so fun times, when we are well and when we don't feel so good, when we have financial wealth or are rich in love alone.

I will honor and respect you always Xander, and never deny that which I can give. I only ask the same in return, as that is the nature of such oaths. I also ask the Gods and Goddesses to grant us perfect love and perfect trust.

Xander, please accept this ring as a symbol of my love. Let it open the door to our future and let darkness forever be in our past. Xander, please say you will marry me and be my husband, forever and two days.

Why I Married A Murderer

His

These Vows I make to you freely and most willingly, with love, honor and a true heart:

I will Love you all of our lives.

I will strive to be all that a husband and partner should be. I will be open, honest and loyal to you always.

That being said, I will not be perfect. I will make mistakes, upset you and hurt your feelings on occasion. I will try to do all of that as little as possible. And I will apologize, probably a lot. Sorry.

I will support you and believe in you always.
Even when we are apart, you will never be alone.
I will treasure and cherish you always.
And I will do my best to make you as proud to have me as your Husband as I am to have you as my wife.

I have searched for you all of my life, and am blessed that you found me.

My heart to thee
My body to thee
Hand fasted and Heart joined
So Mote It Be!

So on September 22, 2006, Mabon, a pagan holiday even, we were married. No, there is no special *something-something* for this type of occasion in Nevada either. We were allowed only a brief kiss to consummate it. We celebrated by sharing two vending machine one-tier hostess cupcakes.

Moving Closer to the Truth

I had been getting fairly involved in public meetings related to the prison system. I attended as many as I could and always had something prepared for public comment. I had become an advocate.

I preferred the word advocate over activist. Activist seems so aggressive and potentially violent: "There was a demonstration today where *activists* were out of control; police were called and pepper spray was used to contain them"—that was the idea I had in my head when I thought of the word activist. *I* wasn't doing anything that warranted the use of pepper spray. I wasn't out agitating people's nerves, or getting in people's faces. I was simply expressing my thoughts and concerns, passionately, but professionally. I was neither wholly right nor wholly left—and I made that point every now and then when I sat on the fence with some issues.

I had some experience with the justice system prior to my involvement with Xander. I had been the victim of my brother's *unbrotherly* (to say the least) actions and felt the justice system had not been nearly hard enough on him. They never actually "labeled" him a violent person, much less charged him appropriately. The police were usually called *due* to a violent incident, but for some reason, the eventual charge was always non-violent (usually because he had stolen property—clearly visible—like a dump truck in the front yard; and, no, I'm not even making that up as an example).

Then there are people in prison charged for violent crimes that they were accessories in, and did not actually commit the violent act, but were now labeled a violent person and sentenced/housed accordingly. This was the case with my husband who, while not completely innocent, was in the wrong place at the wrong time when a murder occurred by someone else's hand. Nevada is one of only six states that still have the felony murder rule on the books. We, as in the United States, got the bright idea for this law from England who was smart enough to come to their senses and abandon the law many years ago. We still have six states that haven't caught up yet and are still wasting taxpayers money and people's lives on a ridiculous law.

The proper labeling of an inmate was one of my biggest issues as an advocate because it involved a lot of government spending to lock people up for a very long time for choosing the wrong people to hang around—people who are most likely not a threat to society at all. Yet, people like my brother who *was* very violent and/or addicts would be sentenced to short term stints, get out, and often wreak more havoc. I knew keeping them in longer wasn't necessarily the answer, but there must be a better way to spend $20,000+/year of taxpayers' money to rehabilitate (fix) them.

It saddened me as the economy took a dump that we were losing teachers and government programs because we had to keep "violent" people locked up for 10 years or more when they didn't really commit the actual violent act, and others kept getting out and going right back to dope, stealing, or worse. Okay, off my soapbox before I write a book within a book!—which I could do!—and, hey, maybe I will!

[**Editor:** You should.]

***

I liked my job as a Records Analyst (I commonly referred to myself as an ANAL-yst; if you know anyone in that profession, you'll understand). However, I despised most of the people in my department; and I'm sure the feeling was mutual. Our department had the nickname "The Fashion Show," which I think actually made our manager proud. It was an utter embarrassment to those of us who actually wanted to take pride in our work, our accomplishments, and our contributions to the organization as a whole, and not be known solely for "looking pretty." Most days I just wanted to puke when "looking good" was the emphasis rather than "doing good" work. Eventually, it generated almost regularly-scheduled heated arguments with my boss. Although we worked well together 90% of the time, we learned through a personality test that the entire department was forced to undergo, that she had a need to *look* right while I had a need to *do* right. Regardless of who was right or wrong, I had to exit stage left.

I got a contract consulting position in Reno and was thrilled to get out of Las Vegas (again). I was glad to be making more money and being paid to *do* a job, not look pretty. Most of all, I was delighted to move closer to my new husband. I would also be closer to Carson City, our state capital, so I could get even more involved in public meetings. I learned a lot during that time about politics. I also learned a lot from people related to the subject of criminal justice, whether by appointment, election, employment, or by concerned citizen and family members.

Xander almost despised the fact that I was going to these meetings. I don't think he liked the attention he was getting inside because I was actually doing well. I believe there was an envy or jealousy issue from the other inmates whose families or support systems on the outside either didn't care enough to make any kind of effort for them, or went about trying to help their loved ones inside with such combative methods that they caused more harm than good. Observing some of these family members who acted so obnoxiously and disrespectfully to the elected officials in public meetings, I often could clearly see how their sons or daughters could end up in prison. Occasionally I wondered if I would rather see the parent locked up *with* their kid, or maybe even just swap them for a minute or two. There were times that it was frightening to see how venomous these parents could be to another person in public.

About the same time that I moved to Reno, Xander had moved from Nevada State Prison to Warm Springs Correctional Center just down the road (where the pastor showed up on our first attempted wedding day).

This was a GREAT move for him—or so I thought. Warm Springs had been a minimum facility for years, but they had recently bumped it up to medium because they had to accept more medium custody inmates due to overcrowding. The move made it likely that at his next parole hearing he might be viewed as a minimum custody inmate and hopefully get paroled to his second and final sentence of 5-20 years.

He had been at the same State Prison for several years, so he was very accustomed to how things ran there, the people, the inmates, the yard rules, etc. It would seem to most of society that it would be good to now be around minimum custody people and not the more violent and scary medium/max types, right? Wrong. The general public does not realize that the lower level offenders (the short timers) are really the cancer of our society.

We are all too excited to let out the druggies and petty thieves in favor of those scary violent people, until they move next door and break into our homes, to steal our shit to buy more dope. Whereas, the horrible violent person may have committed one violent act out of passion, fear, pressure, etc., and it may have been a situational event rather than a habitual pattern. Habitual, meaning habit, as in it is repeated over and over, like drug addicts and theft crimes, in case it's not clear.

Now that Xander was being placed with a much more scumbag crowd who had not done the time to really kick their 'habits' (many of which continued, if not got worse inside), he was miserable. He missed the long-timers who had done the time and learned the meaning of respect, often just to survive. He also had a hard time with the staff, who like much of society, judged long-timers as being violent people that should receive harsher treatment. Little did they know how respectful the long-timers had learned to become, unlike the punk ass dope heads that were in and out of prison like a revolving door. Ok, off the soap box again, sorry.

***

Actually, since I'm half covered in suds anyway (and the bubbles have me reflecting on that time...)—it dawns on me now that I whole-heartedly threw myself into being an advocate, not only trying to bring attention to anything that might help Xander, but also to fix the incredibly broken Justice System. Why this compulsion? As I've said, I never really thought I was hiding behind my fat all those years when I *was* fat—it was who I was. However, looking back, I see that perhaps I was now trying to take on a new identity since the fat girl was gone. Like a superhero trying on a new pair of spandex to see how it fits—get it? (yeah, me neither; the idea of a former fat girl fighting against the broken Criminal Justice System doesn't really go with the whole "superhero" image—but I still thought it was a funny visual). I was never one to think small, so I guess taking on the Justice System seemed like a big enough nemesis to latch on to, so to speak.

***

I really liked being in Reno, at first. I liked being closer to Xander. I liked not spending $300 on gas and hotels, not to mention the time those 800+ miles round trip took through the ugly desert every month or so. I initially moved into a crappy part of town but I liked it.

Xander had heard horror stories about this part of town and wanted me to move immediately. When I told him where I rented a place, he said, "Most of the people I know in here are from that part of town, which tells me you need to move, *now*!"

Xander wrote to my mother-hen friend and asked him to come up and check it out for him. My friend reported back to Xander that I had chosen well within the little area, and I was just fine, so he let up on insisting that I move. I think it was really Xander that wanted to move. Because I was now so much closer, I started visiting every weekend and I was pretty darn happy about it. But that happiness was pretty short lived. I don't know if it was his move to the other facility or if he just couldn't put on the act of being a happily married man that often. I swear, little asshole critters started coming out of his skin through his words and his actions.

Why else would he be such a jerk when I gave up every Saturday and Sunday along with $20 in quarters each visit so we could eat the vending machine crap? I tried visiting just every other week, but that didn't improve things either. I actually began to dread the visits even though they were now only 30 miles away and I could be back home to sleep in my bed every night. Even though the visits got him away from the scumbags, as he called them, for a few hours, it was becoming all too clear that he dreaded our visits too.

Xander started pressuring me a bit that it was time I grew up and settled down, meaning buy a house and sit still. I was 42 at the time, so it probably wasn't a bad idea. I had a few permanent jobs, whatever that word means in this generation's job market; but for the most part, I enjoyed contract work. Contract jobs were great money while they lasted, and they forced me to stay flexible in case I had to move to another state for a few months or longer. I enjoyed the idea of being paid to take a vacation in other places and discover different areas as a local vs a tourist. However, maybe it *was* time to grow up now and plant some roots.

So I bought a house.

Xander was actually a big part of the process as I sent him pictures, descriptions, etc. of houses I considered in my price range. The house I ended up buying, I actually initially just saw from the outside and I didn't really like it. The back yard had a drastic steep slope to it, which I thought was a waste of property, not to mention a potential flood nightmare. Xander saw the pictures I sent and said the slope would be perfect for his gardening plans. He gave me a different perspective about it by suggesting layered tiers. Based on his ideas and plans, and it being the right price at the time, I bought it.

The previous owners had paid $280k for it so I thought I was getting a sweet deal at $205k. My client at the time, an economics major, told me to wait; he thought we hadn't hit bottom on the housing market yet. I talked to my client's CFO who held my contract and I asked how secure my job was. He assured me that I was in the budget for another year and a half. I bought the house. The economy immediately took a nosedive, and I was let go one month after the house closed.

I had no income and $1,500 a month mortgage so I got really creative while I looked for work over the next 11 months. Luckily, I had some money saved (thank you, mother-hen friend for making me do that) and I wasn't afraid of much.

I went to storage unit auctions before they got popular, and I actually got lucky with a few. I used the reason (excuse) of money conservation to trim down my visits to Xander even more, which he didn't seem to mind at all. He may have even suggested it, I don't remember. I took the time I was not working to re-do all the landscaping and fix up the house. Everyone thought I was crazy because they thought I would lose it (the house, not my mind. Most people thought I lost my mind when I married Xander.)

I wanted to think positively and use my off time productively. I did an amazing job, if I do say so myself. But I finally ran out of money, exactly one month before I got a new contract job. The bank refused to work with me for that one stink'n month, because I was not yet employed, so I put the house up for short sale. It sold in less than 24 hours, largely due to the new landscape and other improvements I did, but for almost half what I paid for it.

Pardon Me

I got a contract job just south of San Francisco, which put even more distance between Xander and me. Though it was only four hours away instead of the eight that Vegas was, the fact that I was there for 2-3 weeks at a time was enough to justify visiting him even less. We never really fought about anything in particular, what could we, really? So we just made personal attacks at each other.

***

Why I Married A Murderer

T,

I'm sorry, but I just can't deal with your neurosis and bi-polar mood swings any longer. I thought I could, but it's just too much. Your anger, rage and incomprehension is driving me to distraction. It's obvious that no matter what I say or do, it'll never be good enuff for St. Teresa, the perpetual victim. I sincerely believe you need help.

Maybe I have been pushing you away because I'm afraid to speak to you, or to write. Communicating with you is like navigating a mine field – and you scare me. You go right ahead and blame me for everything because reality has very little meaning for you. Now you can go and tell everyone they were so right about me. You are clearly no more the woman I married-than I am the man you did. Nor are you a woman I wish to be married to. You never got screwed, but you'll never be able to see that. That's really sad and I feel very bad for you. Please try and find some help.

***

We were going a week or so between phone calls and even *they* became dreaded. They were so cold, heartless, and painful, and trust me, *we both* felt like we were navigating landmines. He was absolutely right that I had adopted bi-polar mood swings. What he always failed to admit, was that they were often in direct response to his emotional cruelty, complete disrespect, and total unappreciation for anything I did. We were just about to throw in the towel. Our unspoken plans to split came to a screeching halt when our attorney called and said he was selected for the Pardon's Board.

151

Approximately 1,800 inmates apply to be heard by the Pardon's Board and about 10-14 lucky ones are chosen. Being chosen in itself is like winning the lottery. The real stress comes when only a few, at best, get any action (results). They hope for the best, but plan for the ultimate gut shot. Most return back to their cells with their head hung low and soul beaten down.

Xander getting selected for the Pardon's Board was the ultimate payday for all the work I had put in over the past years attending meetings, preparing white papers and reports, rubbing elbows, and hiring an awesome attorney—which didn't hurt either. I called the prison and asked to speak to the woman in charge of the department he worked in. I was petrified scared, as this is a HUGE no-no. You do NOT try to call an inmate no matter what! I spoke to her as sweetly and politely as I could muster. I said, "I know this is not acceptable, but Xander just made the Pardon's Board, and I am sure you can understand how important that news would be to him... so if you could please just ask him to call me as soon as he is able to, that would be super appreciated."

He called me on his next break and was *pissed*. He started right in on how much trouble he could be in right now because of *this little stunt*, and continued to berate me for saying that it was a cheap shot to get back at him for "not being the perfect husband," etc.. It was a pretty safe assumption his boss didn't tell him the reason I called so I could have the "honor" of telling him myself. I finally cut him off with, "Honey, honey, honey, you made the Pardon's Board." Dead Silence.

"Did you hear me? Honey, we did it! You made the Pardon's Board!" I could feel the total overwhelming emotion he must have been feeling; the relief, the joy, the fear. I'm sure his heart stopped for a moment and he was heading into a cold sweat at 90 miles an hour. I could have never guessed in my wildest imagination his response when he finally spoke, "I suppose you are going to sabotage my chances for actually getting it now that we're not getting along." I was absolutely floored that he could think that, let alone say it. Then it was *my* heart that had stopped for a moment.

Now was not the time to have marriage issues so I curbed the boiling anger I had building up inside. Of course, I wanted to totally explode with something like, "How could you even THINK that after all I have done to get us here?" I was proud of myself for taking the higher road, at least this once, and said, "Whether we are married or not, or even together, does not change the fact that you should not be in prison. You have done more than enough time for your involvement in a crime and you don't need to be sucking up any more taxpayer's dollars. I will not give up now, and I will see this through, to the best of my ability. I will do *everything* in my power to help the attorney, and help your chances of success."

He seemed relieved. I think more so that I didn't explode back at him, which I'm sure he expected, and I'm also sure was the very reason he made the jab in the first place. This was what our relationship had been like since I moved to Reno; him saying shit to get a reaction out of me so he could say I was crazy for getting so upset; it was total mind fuckery at its best.

People in prison are interesting creatures. You may have heard the term "institutionalized"—well, it's a word that explains the mentality that Xander had developed in prison. He immediately got scared of that all-too-likely gut shot and wanted to avoid that pain by just taking the blow now and giving up all hope. Hope is a very dangerous thing to have in prison, or so I'm told.

However, I refused to let him give up hope now. We made the Pardon's Board list. It was time to sprint to the checkered flag!

I requested and received over 30 letters of support including one from an Assemblyman from Las Vegas with whom I had developed great rapport. His step-brother, who was a police officer at the time, wrote a letter of support; a huge risk and possible conflict of interest for him (in more than one sense). I even got one of Xander's ex-girlfriends to write a letter of support (the one that *didn't* really die in a car accident).

I was so honored that five people gave up an entire day of their lives (you could never trust the agenda due to control issues with the inmates/security) to sit on uncomfortable bench seats all day in a show of support for my husband.

Our attorney gave his pitch: it was perfect. Xander spoke on his own behalf; his speech was perfect. We stood up when the attorney gestured, and we declined making statements, just as he recommended; we were perfect. Even the District Attorney was soft on him.

After hearing several other cases already, 90% of them being rejected, we had figured out the panel's patterns. They would listen, question in a defensive manner to justify their upcoming negative vote, and then start the voting, usually on the tail end of an attacking question to set the "no's" rolling. The pattern started out no different with Xander.

One member of the panel questioned the Parole Board's decision to give him not one, but two dumps (denials) on his first sentence, the murder charge. "He should have been eligible at 10 [to be paroled to his next sentence]. Any reason that there were five extra years?" The response came from the Parole Board, which I will lightly paraphrase for brevity: "It was more *appealing* to the Parole Board to see him do more time based on the crime. Five extra years seems to be a good average. It was not because of behavior or any disciplinaries that he was denied." Perfect response for us, but a clear gut shot to the taxpayers who just spent $100,000 for five *extra* years because it was more "appealing" to the Parole Board. Now you see how *insane* our Criminal Justice System can get, as he is just one of many.

One of the panel members recognized the typical line of questioning designed to start the 'no' votes rolling—and to our surprise, he headed it off at the pass. He interrupted the pattern we had seen all day by making a positive statement about Xander; how he had already done his time (all of it, as he had done the minimum of both of his sentences). He then started the voting with a "YES, to Grant." It was quickly seconded. My stomach dropped with a thunk and Xander probably just shit his pants. The voting continued. "Yes", "Yes", "Yes", "Yes", "Yes", "Yes", "Yes", "No", "Yes".

"Motion carries."

OH MY GOD, WE DID IT!!!

I was visibly shaking, like a monkey on crack, but in a happy and good way. A curtain came over me that instant—was this a dream? No, no way... This *never* happens at the Pardon's Board; I had already attended a few in the past so I knew what to expect; little or nothing. Wake up! Wake up! How could you fall asleep at a time like this? I turned to my friends on each side of me for confirmation that I was sleeping. I expected to see my friend's faces drooped down and half asleep as they were much of the day waiting for Xander's case. The second jolt came when they too looked like little monkey's on crack, shaking with excitement. Oh my God, we did it! He's coming home! He's really coming home!

HE had three weeks to prepare to leave the only home he knew for the last 16 years of his life. *I* had three weeks to get the house in order (which wasn't too tough because I had worked hard to make his presence known there long before). The real challenge was that *we* had three weeks to figure out how to fall in love again....

THREE SHORT WEEKS!

***

He walked out the gate on December 22nd, another Pagan holiday—Winter Solstice. After having breakfast, with real metal utensils, a bit of clothes shopping, and seeing his Parole Officer, we were finally home. We had a fairly blissful month or so and then the asshole critters, who went dormant for a 30-day hibernation period, reared their ugly heads again.

I was able to work from home for a few months during the time Xander was just released, so we were together 24/7. This seemed like a good idea at first to help him reconnect with society and get our love groove back. It's hard to imagine how much changes in just 16 years. He had never seen the Internet, never held a cell phone, and had no clue how to pay for gas at the pump, or experienced the joy of cash back using a debit card at the store.

He had convinced me over and over during our *new relationship energy* (NRE) years that he would have no problem getting along with me, no matter what, after all the scumbags he'd had to live with in close quarters all those years—I would be a piece of cake, he would always say. However, our bizarre fights over the stupidest shit, or nothing at all, even before he came home, would indicate otherwise.

We both seemed to be thankful when I went back to work at the job site four hours away and was gone for two weeks at a time again. This gave *me* time to think about how much I really loved him and how badly I wanted this to work—and it gave him time to realize how much he wanted other women.

The Beginning of the End

I was having hormone problems. That's it. *That's why* I had been so emotional and *that's the reason* I'd been overreacting when he constantly fucked with my head trying to convince me that *I* was crazy. It was because of my hormones! Those little chemicals racing from one cell to another in my body! They were all out of whack! Who'd a thunk it???

Yeah, really. Well, that's what *he* said anyway.

Xander kept telling me that because of my age (I was 42 at the time), I was going through "changes" and because he *cared sooooo much,* he wanted me to go to the doctor and get on some medication for *my* problem.

KA-*chunk!* That was the sound of my axles breaking. I could *feel* it. Another diagnosis from the man I loved! Thanks, hubby—now, audience, tell us what she's won! A brand... NEW...*BROKEN HEART!*

Is there anything in the world worse than being told you're all fucked up on account of something that's beyond your control?—yet that some quack in a street corner office downtown has the cure for? I mean—c'mon!

He treated me like I was an annoying fly that wouldn't go away, and yet I would feel so guilty for getting upset about feeling that way. I often cried and begged him to tell me what I could do, anything, to make him feel more comfortable in his transition back into society. And all he could say was, "Teresa, your hormones are all fucked up. You need to see a doctor. These problems are all in your head. *Really.*"

Yet sometimes, according to Xander, it wasn't my hormones at all, but it was just simply 'me'. I remember one time, I was sitting at the table sobbing and he was standing against the couch with his arms folded in front of him in such a God-like and condescending way, while proceeding to tell me everything *I* was doing was wrong and what *I* could do to improve *myself* so that *our* relationship *would* work.

He had all the answers—except the one that mattered. The simplest thing—a little TLC. Just a few short inches of love would have lasted me miles.

Although he would rarely go anywhere or do anything with me, he actually accompanied me to the doctor "to show his support" of me getting better. I spoke with the doctor at great lengths about how I was feeling and how it must be a hormonal imbalance or something because I just felt so horrible. She listened patiently and when I was finally finished, she said, "You don't have a *hormone* problem, you have a *husband* problem."

Well—that was a relief. Or so I thought! Since she didn't have a pill to fix husbands, she put me on antidepressants! Uh, thanks Doc!

Okay—so they helped a little (but I don't think they make any strong enough to send you into the oblivion you require to avoid the emotional abuse making you depressed in the first place—and I don't know that I really *wanted* oblivion). But even as I had to wait two weeks for the meds to help lift my mood, the sexual side effects kicked in by day three; no orgasm. I switched to another kind which allowed me to make my "o" face, but they made me even more depressed. I couldn't win.

There were moments of clarity, but they were few and far between. Sometimes I really *did* know it wasn't me, and in fact, *he* was the problem. I would hear him telling other women on the phone, in very loving and caring tones, how *they* could use herbs and other pagany things to cure their ailments, even depression and hormone issues. I asked him once, "Why don't you help me by using all this knowledge you have about herbs? Why are you helping *other* women with natural remedies and not your own wife?" He would snidely respond with, "I have *tried* to help you but you don't listen – *they* listen and *they* take my advice because *they* know that I *do* know what I'm talking about. *You* don't listen because you don't believe me and don't trust me, which is very sad and unfortunate." Even though he <u>never</u> told me jack about herbs…Poof! There went my brief moment of clarity; I was back to being broken again. Ka-*chunk*— there go my wheels!

Another little mind-fuck was his "art" work. There is no question that he was a fantastic artist. However, 99% of his art was creating images of beautiful women and pagan type stuff. I had tried to sell his art for years before he came home. People enjoyed looking at it, but it wasn't the kind of stuff you could actually take home and put on your wall—unless you were a dirty old man, living alone in a trailer—like the kind you might see in a B Horror movie. He also had no less than a dozen beautiful women tattooed on his body. It seemed everywhere I turned; I was competing against all these other women in his life, for his love and attention.

He would always refer to it as "art" to insinuate that I wasn't thinking of all these other women in the proper context. He would say shit like I shouldn't compare myself to them because "this room could be *full* of beautiful women but you would still be the most beautiful to me." Yeah, this is my point, as "crazy" as it is…. I can't JUST BE the most beautiful woman in the world to him—he has to *fill* the fucking room *full* of beautiful women WITH me, and THEN I am the most beautiful woman in his life! Grr! Ka-*chunk*! Ka-*chunk*! Ka-*chunk*!

There were many things he said and did that were clearly intended to indicate that I was not anywhere near what was most important to him. He would remind me in interesting ways that *his* feelings and *his* desires should be my priority at all times; as long as whatever I did to help or please him didn't interfere with *his privacy*, of course.

He also often made very adamant points, unprompted and completely unnecessary, that his religion was more important to him than I was, and that I was to never stand in the way of it. That pretty much put *others* in his religion in a more important position than me too. He painted pagan symbols to help and heal others but I was sitting right there and he couldn't give two shits about helping or healing me, other than pointing out how wrong my thinking was about everything. He would hold these alter clothes in his hands so delicately, and share this "knowledge" about healing and helping through his pagan path, offering it so freely to everyone but me. He always told me that I needed to take responsibility for myself: "Only *you* can help yourself," he would say constantly—even though he never ran out of ways to point out how broken I was and therefore *incapable* of helping myself. Yet somehow, all these other pagan girl friends of his who needed *his* help so much didn't need to help *them*selves; *they* were part of his "community" after all and I clearly was *not*.

The funny part was that I *was* very involved in the pagan community before he got out. I gave up a huge chunk of my life to help him while he was in prison to be more comfortable, and I also did everything I could to help his transition when he got out. I threw myself into communities that I knew he would want to be a part of and spoke very highly of him so they would accept him with open arms when he came home.

I did everything in my power to get him out of prison—and I succeeded. I defended him to everyone—to family, friends, politicians, people in the pagan and artist communities, and even to *his* family. Yet, when he came home, time after time, he held his time, his efforts, and his power with a clinched fist, at arm's length away from me for pure mental torture, while I wept, practically begging to be loved. He would often put me down while he praised and defended his friends, friends he had just met and known only a few weeks—friends who had *not* stood by him nor helped him gain his freedom. Hell, most didn't even know him until he got out and yet somehow they ranked higher than I did in his book. I could never wrap my head around how I had defended *him*, a convicted murderer and kidnapper, to so many *important* people in my life, but somehow I ranked below his trailer trash (literally) friends.

At the time, because he had me half way to the nut ward anyway, I would think, "I have shown you a million ways how much I love you .... If I am not worth YOU showing me just a little of how much I mean to you, why would I think *I* am worth *MY* time to care and love myself?"

When I would try to "help myself" and get self-help CDs or books, he would roll his eyes at them as if to say they were rubbish. When I tried to share some little gem of information that I thought was helpful, he would dismiss it, and me, with a cold shrug of his shoulder and return to his instant message chats with his girl-friends.

I had even made arrangements with a wonderful author and friend of mine, G. Brian Benson (real name—look him up, he's awesome!), to talk about 'balance' with us. Brian had written a few inspirational books and was doing workshops at the time, but I was always out of town working—so he offered to do a personal workshop just for us the next time I was home, just two blocks from our house. Xander refused to go with me.

I was the one with the problem after all, not him. *He* didn't need to hear any of this "crap," as he called it—*he* was perfect, and I was far from it. *That* was the message he sent me with his rolling eyes and rude remarks about how he didn't know anything about this guy and had no interest in meeting him. This was the first time I realized how "love" really meant two entirely different things to us.

I had gotten four people who knew nothing about Xander to drive 60 miles round trip to attend his Parole Hearing. I had gotten five people to give up an *entire* day of their lives to attend his Pardon's Board Hearing; not to mention countless other people, including an assemblyman, who didn't *know* him from Adam, to write letters on his behalf to support efforts to grant his pardon. These people trusted me, trusted my feelings and my judgment—and yet my husband didn't trust my feelings or judgment enough to agree to meet ONE man TWO blocks from our house for ONE hour? What the fuck was wrong with me that he couldn't love *me* just that tiny little bit to try to help me for one fucking hour of HIS life when so many people who didn't even know him had helped him (for me)?

He was beautiful—beautiful like his artwork. He was complete, whole, and happy, as I *should* have been. I was selfish to want and need *so much* of him and was barely a speck of dust to his whole, beautiful, perfect self. I was broken and imperfect in every way. I had no talents, no skills, no passion.... Just alone and broken. Of course, I know better now, but at the time, these were thoughts that were spoon fed to me and for some reason I swallowed them whole. I fell right into his plan to make the failure of our relationship my fault.

The other women, though, they WERE my fault. I had this idea that I wanted to be a "good, loving, caring wife" and let him make up for some lost time while he was in prison. I told him he could "play" with two girls I knew. I had different reasons for choosing each of them, which I thought at the time were good ones. Both were very familiar with polyamory as well as the swinger lifestyles, therefore they both knew very well the difference between "poly" and "play", as well as the boundaries of the "permission" that was offered. One of them took me up on the offer. She and Xander had sex. Everything about the "event" was totally open and honest. The night, as far as I know, went totally ok, and I never had a problem with the sex part.

It was the insanely psycho behavior on her part that followed that night that was the next mind-fuck. She became completely obsessed with Xander. Making not-so-discreet posts on Facebook and Yahoo, calling, texting, e-mailing, writing totally psycho poetry; it was almost four months of total hell to scrape her off of us like a 10-ton emotional leach.

Even after three months, her husband, who also knew and was ok with the sex part, called me at work begging me to talk to her; "She won't stop crying—she doesn't know what she did wrong." OMG! *SHE* needs medication more than I ever did. How about the fact that she simply would not leave us alone, despite our repeated, and ignored, requests. She was married (for like 20 years), had two kids, friends, and chickens and goats to feed to keep her busy, and she wouldn't stop crying for three months after she fucked my husband ONE night? WTF? Xander finally realized she was insane and told her we would get a restraining order if she didn't leave us alone. Then her friend took her place in psycho city.

*****

Her friend started "hanging out" at our house when I was out of town working for two weeks at a time. The first time, that I know of, was on my birthday. I had to drive 20 miles to get cell reception just to call Xander. He told me she just "stopped by." As silly as it might seem, I felt awkward to have interrupted their conversation, so I kept our phone call brief and said I would call back later. I hung out in this little coastal town for a bit, had lunch, and then called back hoping to get some quality time with my husband even if it was only over the phone. This was my first birthday since he'd been out, so it was hard enough that due to my job we were still apart.

Two hours had gone by before I called again, so I was pretty surprised to hear she was still there. It didn't help that he sounded like he had a pretty big smile on his face—and I didn't get the feeling that it was because they were planning a surprise party for me when I got home. I felt even more awkward that I'd called again even though he knew I would be calling back in a while, and he *knew* I didn't have reception where I was staying, and he *knew* I only had a window of time to make the call—and he *knew* it was my FUCKING BIRTHDAY!

One of many other really odd things this woman did: after she had fairly major surgery, she asked MY husband to pick her up from the hospital instead of hers. Xander claimed that her husband had to work to keep their business going so he couldn't. I was thinking, "Why doesn't she have any other friends/family that would be much more appropriate to pick her up after a surgery?" Then the kicker was that she wanted to re-cover at *our* house instead of her own which was extra odd since she lived closer to the hospital then we did, and it was further out of the way for her husband to pick her up. The real icing on the cake was when Xander told me what a dick her husband was in that when he came to pick her up he didn't even park by the door and hardly helped her to the car. I felt like screaming, "A) She should have went to *her* home to recover and B) How would you feel if I wanted another (married) man to pick me up at the hospital instead of you, and *then* I wanted to go to *his* house, instead of *our* bed, while *his* wife is out of town?"

As their "friendship" continued on, she'd send Xander extremely flirty texts, instant messages (the fact that he tried to hide them from me was a dead give-away that they contained content I'd have every right to be pissed off about)—but it was the emails that were the worst. There was one in particular from her telling him that I was his new warden and he was serving another life sentence being married to me. Uh, yeah… because *I* have a problem with two psycho, married, trailer trash bitches that don't have the decency and respect to stay out of *our* marriage, and let us build *our* marriage since he'd only been home a few months? One of these women had been married 20 years and the other was married for 13 years, but for some reason, they were more interested in ensuring that *my* marriage didn't last a minute longer. Ya, it *must* be me!

Sadly, Xander also had me convinced I was the problem because he should be allowed to have *his own* friends. I even heard, "What? I can't have friends over after school until mommy comes home? Is *that* it?"

Oh, the 'poor child'.

***

However, one day Xander did act like a loving and supporting husband while all this bullshit drama was going on. He put his arm around me in a very sweet way and said, "Honey, they are *only* being like that because they *know* it gets to you." I wanted to bask in this brief loving moment—but I lost it when I realized what he was saying. "So you KNOW they *are trying* to mentally torture me, *trying to* SEE me cry and hurt, and you STILL won't put a fucking stop to this?" This resulted in one of Xander's most dramatic eye rolls yet, which told me, "I *try* to love you, but no matter what I try to do to *help* you, you just don't see it." I didn't see it, because I was broken, and his emotional cruelty was the weapon he used to break me.

After about five months of complete emotional hell, *he* finally realized they were both playing tag team to drive a wedge in our marriage and because we were both so sick and tired of speaking their names, they became *un*affectionately referred to by both of us as Crazy #1 and Crazy #2. Shortly after I almost breathed a sigh of relief that the two crazies were *finally* leaving us alone to build our marriage that we should have been allowed to do when he first came home, he started on the Internet shit. He put personal ads online, emailed escorts from Craigslist asking how big their boobs were and if they wanted to hook up, etc.

Did I exist any longer? Was I really just a new warden figure? Did the concept of "wife" mean anything to him?

When I saw these e-mails and confronted him about them, he mind-fucked me again! It really was beautiful! "I did that *on purpose* to see if you would check up on me. See, YOU are worse at 'sneaking around' than I am. How can you yell at me for 'sneaking around' and being untrustworthy when YOU are sneaking around checking on me; I can't trust YOU to let me have a tiny bit of privacy that I have been denied for 16 years but you claim YOU want 'trust' in this relationship?" Yup, I sucked, I was wrong, and I was broken.

Xander gets the square! Ron, tell him what he's won! You bet, Bob! A brand... NEW... *horrible, horrible wife!*

Yep, I was a horrible, horrible wife. How *dare* I have the nerve to be hurt or upset by my husband asking a prostitute how big her boobs are and asking if they could hook up.

I *do* know now, and even did then, that no one can *make* you feel one way or another—at least that's what all the self-help books and shrinks will *tell you* to feel/know 'inside'. My therapist sometimes tried to get away with that crap, too—but I told him, "Listen, Doc, my life is like a pendulum; on one end I KNOW I'm awesome. I'm a Fucking Rock Star.. I KNOW this...and I KNOW it's TRUE... however, not that I'm going to use the word 'validation' God forbid, but IF I am such a Rock Star, which I KNOW I am.. Then WHY is THIS how people treat me (as I would swing my arm almost violently to the other side indicating the swing of the pendulum)". To which my Doc would reply, "Well, Teresa, sometimes even Rock Stars get the blues...." My therapist is a fucking poet; right? Yeah, but at the time, no matter how hard I tried to remember how awesome I was, how strong I was, how smart I was, I somehow allowed my husband to make me feel small and insignificant in his world full of other and more important women.

Note: For those of you last few completely honest, devoted, faithful monogamous folks out there who are shaking your head and tsk-ing me thinking (or even yelling at this chapter, which would be kinda weird, but who am I to judge?) That I "asked for this" by allowing my husband to have sex with another woman, even if it was only once, let me respond. I personally can't stand Harley Davison motorcycles or the lifestyle that many who love them live by. I hear they are the nicest people and stick together and help each other out when in need, but most of what I see are fat-gutted, vest-wearing, obnoxious, bearded freaks and their skinny, lacy tank top wearing, bleach blonde, bandana wear'n chicks (who may or may not have 'fell off' if you believe their t-shirts) riding their ridiculously loud bikes hurting my eardrums... but again, I hear they are nice folks.

Likewise, I don't understand how some Christians can go to church, speak the good word about Jesus, and then trash talk their neighbors, step over homeless people in America, on their way to convert people in Zimbabwe, to the way of the Lord...but I hear they are nice folks too. My point is, those who are in the Polyamory and/or Swinging Lifestyles know and understand the "rules" of those lifestyles, and while I don't understand the creed of the biker lifestyle, nor the morals of organized religions, I don't expect someone who is convinced their marriage is monogamous (and, statistically speaking, 70% aren't), to understand the respect and trust that *most* people in the Poly/Swing lifestyles *do* maintain.

But trust me, what happened with these two crazy bitches was fucked up.

And then if these women he just met, and the women in his artwork, weren't enough to fuck my head up... there was always his religion which drove a wand, I mean a wedge, between us.

***

Xander was Wiccan and an artist, so when I moved to Reno, I threw myself in both of those circles to feel closer to him. I *do* love art anyway, and I was curious about paganism so that wasn't a stretch either. Even though I knew I would *never* jump in with both feet, I could "see" parts of their beliefs—and they do have a good hearted and caring community. Anyway, I went to many of their religious holiday events such as Beltane which was a 2-3 day camp out; I attended two years in a row before Xander came home. I took pictures and wrote letters telling him all about it so he could feel like he was there, and fit in better when he came home. When he came home, I was soooo excited to share that event with him, to take the back seat if you will, to let him lead and show me his pagan side. Again, I was never that into the religion part of it, for me, but I so badly wanted to 'respect his path'.

So, the year he came home and we could be there together, you can imagine how excited I was that they were going to have Beltane fires for the first time since I started going. The idea is, if you are a couple, you jump over the fire together and make a wish (or something like that), and then on the other side, you approach a "wise one" who carefully watched you jump over the fire *together* and gives you a "reading/prediction" of your future *together*.

OKAY?

I was looking forward to jumping over the fire together all day. There were several other "rituals" that were done throughout the weekend that we enjoyed together including preparing for and doing the may pole stuff (it's a very romantic and sexual ritual). We enjoyed the potluck together, visiting with friends, etc…and then finally, after much anticipation, they lit the fires. I stood up to start heading toward the line that was already forming and Xander said, "I don't feel like doing it, but *you* can go ahead if *you* want."

THUNK.

Can you imagine what was going through my head and heart? This is HIS thing… and HE doesn't want to do it…this is a COUPLE thing…and he doesn't want to do it…WHY?

I decided it would shed a bad light on him and the event to throw a fit (which I didn't want to do anyway; I was more hurt than upset) or just start bawling and feel sorry for myself—so I just said 'ok' and went to stand in line by myself. After about 10 minutes, he came to … get this…stand in line with me, while "I" waited to jump…but he still did not want to jump WITH me. It wasn't until the very last minute he decided to jump *with* me. I was happy, yet still so nervous and hurt.

It should come as no surprise, that the "wise one" said we looked "uncomfortable" together and we would have a rough road ahead of us, but he also saw that we *could* get through it if we both wanted it badly enough.

After that… Well, wait, let me back up… I love to camp (and so does Xander)—so I had this tiny little tent that barely fit a queen air bed in it. We slept in that the first night. It was fucking cold! There was condensation that made the walls of the tent freeze—it was like 17 fucking degrees—no kidding. Anyway, so the next day, we left the camp, went into town, and bought a new tent—a super nice, big one. Well, the top was mesh but with a flap over it, so we thought, good, there will be no condensation—well, bad, because it was super fucking cold, with nothing to keep the little body heat we had, in.

Oh…wait, did I say body heat? Ya, this might be a sexually charged pagan holiday AND our first camping trip together, but let's not jump ahead of ourselves here. It was about 10:30pm, the night of the Beltane fires, and I was super tired so *I* went in to bed. *He* sat out by the camp fire—by himself. I waited for like a half hour, but it was sooo fucking cold in there by myself, so I got up and tried to get him to come to bed. He said he wanted to stay up. I said, and totally nicely, I might add, "I think I wanna go home and sleep, and come back early in the morning—it's just way too f'n cold" (we only lived 12 miles away from this "group camp"). To my surprise, he jerked his head around and said, "I hope you don't expect me to go *with* you?" I honestly didn't even think for a minute that he wouldn't—or at the very least say, "Why don't we sit by the fire for a bit and then we will try to go to bed together…or sit by the fire together for a while, and then go home and sleep, together." But, no, he let me drive off that mountain, by myself, alone, go home and sleep, alone, and then come back the next morning.

Did I mention Beltane is a sexually charged holiday? Yes, it's about fucking on the earth to bring fertility to the earth…the may pole is totally representative of a dick…and you wrap ribbons around it to represent the vagina (or so Xander told me in his letters the previous years I went alone). But anyway—ask me if we had sex that whole weekend…go ahead…ask.

I almost begged for it the first night in the tent; he wouldn't budge. Mind you, the previous two years I camped with this group he said shit like "I can't wait to experience that with you so we can make love on Mother Earth" and blah, blah...and then he was sooo fucking cold to me. He didn't even say, "C-c-call me to l-l-let me know you made it off the mountain and home s-s-safe". When I came back early the next morning hoping for some morning wood...I got nothing. He gave me the cold shoulder again. I just wasn't sure witch (pun intended) husband he was anymore—the man I thought I knew and visited for years, or this warlock!

A Chance for a Fresh Start

During an instrumental portion of the song "Love Rollercoaster" by The Ohio Players, a high-pitched scream is heard. The scream was actually done by Billy Beck, but one urban legend has it that it was the voice of someone being murdered while the tape was rolling. Another story told was that it was a girl screaming to her death while falling off a rollercoaster and somehow someone recorded it. Both stories seem ridiculous to me, however I *was* more than ready to take a flying leap off this rollercoaster from hell and scream to *my* death!

My contract job ended and I landed a job in Northern Idaho. It was in a town that I had visited when I was young and also several times as an adult. I always loved this town so I thought it was fate that this job came up

175

just when we needed a fresh start somewhere new. The company insisted on flying both Xander and me up for the interview to make sure he would like it there. He took a break from chatting with girls online long enough to look up information about this little town and he loved everything he saw and read about it. There was a huge lake where he could fish, a mountain nearby he could ski, it was the town I fell in love with as a kid, and it was in the Northwest where we both wanted to be.

He had lived in Washington with his ex-wife and I had lived in Oregon with my ex-husband, so we both felt that Idaho was going to be *ours* and this would be the chance we needed to make our marriage work, finally! The anticipation of moving out of Nevada where he had been incarcerated for 16 years, and from which I had tried to escape twice before, had us focused on the hope and possibilities of starting fresh. We even started getting along better knowing we had this opportunity to be free of the drama that had been weighing us down for the past several months. Wait—did I say "weigh us down?" I *meant* sucking us into the core of the earth like quicksand while being strangled and bitten repeatedly by venomous snakes. Yeah, that was more like how I felt.

I moved up with just what I could fit in my Toyota Rav4, which included not much more than some of my clothes and a cot to sleep on. We had already talked to the parole people in Idaho and they assured us it would be no more than 4-6 weeks before he would be approved to transfer his parole, and we would be together again. I started filling up our adorable three-bedroom town-house with gems I found at yard sales and on Craigslist. Xander had actually viewed the townhouse while I was at my interview, *we* decided it was the best deal, and *I* moved into it sight unseen; how's that for trusting him?

It was only a few weeks after I had moved that he was getting ready to go to Burning Man for his first time. He wasn't doing much packing to bring our stuff up to Idaho (from what I gathered in our phone calls), so I drove down (13 hours each way) over Labor Day weekend to *help*. He didn't know I was coming down until he was already at Burning Man. My plan was that I would just go there, pack a bunch of stuff, and be gone before he came home, but I still held a little hope that he would come home early and we could see each other for a bit.

He managed to call from Burning Man somehow and freaked out that I was on my way down. I should have known to just turn around then. When I got to the apartment, it was late since I left after work and drove all night to get there. I walked in and the stench was like a dive bar at 4am. It reeked of cigarette smoke and piss. He promised he was not smoking in the apartment. He even went on and on that *he* didn't want to live in a place that smelt like a bar either. Wow, and yet here we are; every fuckin' thing now reeks like the bottom of a wet ashtray. The couches, the bed, my clothes that were still there, everything... I was so pissed.

Oh, but he didn't just smoke in the apartment, he kindly emptied all his ashtrays in three different trashes *before* he left so there were like 200 cigarette butts permeating in the closed up place for the whole week he had already been gone. He couldn't have at least taken the trash out before he left? I was beyond disgusted and I couldn't even see or think straight, especially after that long drive to *help* him.

So now that he *knows* I am home and that he could leave Burning Man and come home after the burn (Saturday night), we *could* have spent late Saturday night, Sunday, and Sunday night together. Again, he had already been there for a week. Nope. He not only stayed, but he stayed four more days than he had originally planned, and some other chick decided to stay another four days with him.

Of course, I had to drive all the way back to Northern Idaho to get back to work. Driving while that hurt, pissed, and disappointed, especially 800+ miles on sunflower seeds and Monster energy drinks is not a good combination. By some miracle, I made it home without incident.

A friend of mine called me repeatedly during my first few days back at work in Idaho, asking if I had heard from Xander. Apparently the other chick that decided to stay an extra four days with him had a boyfriend that was calling my friend, asking him to call me, to ask WTF? I almost felt like this guy was attacking me, through my friend, for having a jerk husband who was trying to steal his girlfriend or something. I knew better than to think this girl was a floozy home wrecker. Then again, maybe she was—but I also knew Xander. I felt like I had an open gash across my chest that despite my trying to stitch it up, everyone seemed to be tearing it back open and throwing buckets of salt in the hole.

Meanwhile, I was still dedicated to making this marriage work. I just believed that once he got to Idaho, we could leave Nevada and all its drama behind us. It took the Idaho parole people almost a month just to come "inspect" my place before they would then probably spend another four weeks "deciding." They came just one day before he brought all our possessions up on a trip pass. The timing coincided with the end of our apartment lease in Reno. The plan was, if necessary, that Xander would now stay at a weekly scumbag place in Reno until he got his parole transfer approved.

Two female Parole Officers came to the house and had me show them around. I told them that he was coming the very next day to bring our stuff up and it would be great if he could just stay. They not only made it clear that he could *not* stay, but asked me what I planned to do if they denied him. What? You can't keep a husband and wife apart, I thought!

So Xander brought our stuff up, we had an all too brief one day/two night (too tired for sex) visit. We didn't worry about the no sex part because he would only be going back for a week or two, they would approve his transfer, and he would be back in Idaho for good. We had waited to have sex for five years before he came home, we could wait a few more weeks now. Because he would be back so soon, it also seemed like a good idea to let him take my Rav4 back rather than the U-Haul truck I bought.

We had decided to buy a moving truck rather than rent one. It was going to cost $1,300 to rent one to drive one-way to Idaho or we could buy an older one for $2,200. Xander convinced me it was smarter to buy one because we could use it for a business for him if he couldn't get a job, we could turn it into a cool custom camper, or we could just sell it when we were done with it. I also thought it made sense so I bought the truck.

Less than a week after he returned to Reno, they denied his parole transfer request. The reason for the denial was that I had to live in Idaho six months to claim I was a resident. What bullshit! DMV insists that you are a resident in less than 30 days to make you change over your Driver's License, but it takes a permanent job, a permanent home, AND six months to show the Parole Office I'm "stable" in the community. Good Grief.

I didn't fight for almost five years to get Xander out of prison because I am good at giving up, so I fought this decision from every angle I could. A woman at the main Parole Office for the state politely explained what I needed to do. She said she spoke to the woman in our little town who had denied his transfer and if we resubmitted the request, she assured me he would be up before the holidays. Xander re-filed his transfer request, and two days before Thanksgiving the same woman denied him again, for the same reason.

I was so frustrated, sad, angry, bitter, resentful, and well, you name it, so to keep myself from jumping off a bridge, I threw myself into my job. I was on salary making shit money, but I didn't care. I could be at work and stay busy and keep my mind... Well, busy. I even came in and worked the day after Thanksgiving, shoveling a path to the door; the snow was almost two feet thick. I needed to stay busy.

I would work 10-12 hour days M-F, and then worked at least six hours on Saturdays too. Even though I wasn't upper management, I still had a very high-pressure job. Every Monday morning my staff and I would have a meeting with my boss and she would run down the list of outstanding items and say, "Why isn't this done? Why isn't that done?" It was beyond my control that most of it wasn't done because it rested on other people in other departments not taking action. Yet, it still fell on me and my staff. She knew we had little control over other people, and that we weren't privy to the forecast to really know what the priorities would be, but she didn't care. I wasn't hounding people enough, she would say, or she would spend our precious meeting time re-prioritizing our tasks, only to change them again later in the day and scream, "Why aren't you working on the new priorities!" Before she even announced them to us.

My boss was a witch. A real witch, as in Wiccan, and she made it well known to everyone at work including our external auditors and customers. I was waiting for the day that the cough medicine we were making got screwed up and the headlines would read, "Children's Medicine Poisoned by Witch in Charge of Quality." Not only was she a witch, she was also a bitch, and everyone hated her. Many people asked me to ask her questions *for* them because *they* were afraid of her. Not that she would cast a spell on them or anything—she was just plain mean and would say one thing one day and another the next, if she even waited a whole day to change her mind. Having me in the middle was just one more person to blame when they did it *wrong* (but yet the exact way she told them to, in some cases only moments earlier).

One day, I had it and nearly walked out. She was starting to bring me to tears on a weekly basis. I was fighting with the parole people, dealing with Xander telling me, "It's just getting too hard to stay together," even while I was trying so hard to keep us together; I was trying to keep my*self* together at work and somehow keep up a decent morale with my staff with whom I shared an office—which meant there were no secrets. I was about to lose it soon if I didn't cut something loose, and my job seemed the most logical thing to let go at the time.

I hadn't really thought about what I would do after I walked out. I knew I would have been crazy to return to Nevada to live with Xander in his weekly place and subject myself to the white-trash-disrespectful-bitch drama down there, but this was a small town and I had nothing really to keep me here, no major bills other than rent, no car payment, hum... I was tired of driving the U-Haul around town and I had paid off the Rav4 way before Xander came home from prison. I needed a bill; a reason to not just walk out and quit my job.

So that night I bought a brand new Corolla.

**

Xander came up for Christmas. When he came to pick me up from work, I proudly introduced him to many of my co-workers. They were all very happy to meet him, as they knew of our struggles to stay together; you can't keep secrets long in a small company or a small town. When we got home, I noticed there was a big Christmas bow on the door and lights on the front of the porch. "Wow, someone's been busy today, I see." I said with a big heartfelt smile. We walked in, and there was a little Christmas tree in the corner. He said, "I bought decorations, but I wanted to wait and decorate the tree together."

We had a very pleasant time putting the tree together and after dinner we watched a movie. After the movie, I wanted to go to bed and *finally* make love. He wanted to watch *another* movie and finish off *another* bottle of wine, by himself. Our first chance to make love in five months, and yet I went to bed alone.

In just the few days he was there for Christmas, I found text messages on his phone to some chick telling her she is beautiful. There was a picture of her on his phone with her contact information; she was super fat and had so much make up on that she looked like a clown. I asked him why he was telling her she was beautiful. I didn't even know this girl and, of course, I had never even heard him speak of her.

He said she came into his work for a kids-day event to paint their faces and that they had just started talking. (I could see how she would be qualified to paint faces by the way she painted her own.) He went on to say she was having boyfriend troubles so he just told her she is beautiful "to make her feel better about herself." I then later saw very flirty emails to his lesbian friend, who I had briefly heard about, but was never *allowed* to meet. He said he was just being nice to her because her boyfriend just broke up with her and he was trying to make her feel better. Um…A) does anyone else see a pattern here, and B) since when do lesbians have boyfriends?

When I confronted him about the boyfriend/lesbian thing, he quickly said she goes both ways. Hum. He refused to discuss the matter any further so I e-mailed her myself. Turns out, she is *not* gay and he just told me that so I wouldn't be so suspicious about how much he was flirting with her.

The last straw was the day after Christmas when I learned that he was still talking to this super trailer-trash chick who was a well-known home wrecker. She had previously tried to break up a relationship of a friend of mine because she wanted *her*, and wanted her boyfriend out of the picture, she *really did* swing both ways. She was as strange as she was conniving. When I confronted him and asked what he could possibly be talking to this woman every day about, when *we* weren't even talking every day at that point, he packed his bag and said, "I can't handle this anymore—take me back to the airport."

It was the day after Christmas, and the day before his daughter and her friends planned to come up to spend time with us. It would have been the first time he had seen her since he'd been released from prison (a year prior). I knew deep down inside a big part of him leaving then was because he couldn't face his daughter knowing what a crappy father AND shitty husband he really was, but of course he made it all *my* fault.

Working so hard to support him while he was in prison, working so hard to get him out, working so hard to get him out of Nevada and up to Idaho so we could be together, and somehow not being as important to him as these trailer-trash girls *he* just met, had me about ready for a straightjacket.

It was all I could do to put one foot in front of the other and keep moving forward. I was way beyond feeling that I wasn't "good enough" no matter what I did for either my husband or my boss. I worked so hard to get Xander out of prison and succeeded; it was unheard of. Everyone was impressed, amazed, in total awe of my success, except Xander. I totally kicked ass at work, everyone loved me, my staff, production workers and supervisors, top management—everyone but my psycho witch-bitch boss.

The two people I needed the most to appreciate me, and who I tried the hardest to win their respect, were the two that treated me the worst. And what do you know?—they were both witches! Huh, ain't that a kick to the head! Both were supposed to *know* how important respect for your fellow human is. The pagan creed is: "Do as ye will – harm none," yet they were both going out of their way to twist a knife in my heart and mind every day. I had a permanent job in a town I loved and had got my husband out of prison so we could be together, yet I couldn't make sense of what my life had become and I was struggling to find a morsel of happiness to save my life, almost literally.

It was February—the month of Valentine's Day *and* my birthday. I actually thought about holding on through the month. Maybe he would come around and use the opportune events of this month to proclaim his love for and finally put forth some effort to make our relationship work. I came to the painful realization that I was living in more of a fantasy world than the types of women he drew, painted, or had tattooed on his body. In early February, I filed for divorce one day, and quit my job, without notice (for the first time in my life) the very next day. I held up both my middle fingers, and exhaled as though dropping a large weight from my shoulders:

FUCK YOU—BOTH OF YOU!!!

And I felt good....
No, wait, it felt *really* Fucking Good!

But I didn't feel good for long.

Hitting Bottom

The day after I sent the divorce papers to a Private Detective to have him served, Xander sent me the following e-mail (he had no idea the divorce papers were on their way):

This is some of what I have figured out so far.

I am willing to work very hard on:

- *Being much more proactive in sharing information and my life and everything in it with you.*
- *Putting you first in my life ahead of everyone else.*
- *Not being so stubborn and pig headed about things.*

This is what I need you to work on:

- *Treating me as an equal in our relationship.*
- *Realizing that I see things differently than you do and understanding that I do not do everything the same as you, nor should I have to.*
- *Realizing that once you give somebody, anybody, something, it is not yours anymore and not yours to take back.*

Whether you agree that these are issues or not, I feel that they are, and they are issues on my part. If you are willing to start here, then we have a chance of working this out. If not, then I am afraid that there is no hope.

For about a half of a millisecond, I thought maybe I had made a mistake by filing for divorce. In that tiny millisecond, I thought *maybe*, just maybe, he finally did realize he was being an ass and he was actually going to start putting forth an effort of working on our relationship. I didn't even blink twice before I recognized his conniving and conditional loop-holes that would have me in another mind-bender game before you could say, "Straightjacket, but hold the duct tape, please."

The second bullet he pointed out for me, "Realizing that I see things differently than you do and understanding that I do not do everything the same as you, nor should I have to," would pretty much get him out of just about anything. If I had learned anything at all about him by now, this is exactly why he wrote it.

It was not my intention that he was served the divorce papers on Valentine's Day. He was supposed to be served at home, with total discretion, on his day off. It wasn't *my fault* that he ran off to Vegas with his hot, young, tat'd up, roller derby, co-worker, roommate and her metal band boyfriend, in my car. He had no money to help pay *our* bills, or couldn't even contribute a single penny to cover the insurance on the car he was driving, but he somehow had money to take time off work and take people to Vegas. He could have fun with *them*, but refused to have fun with me the one time *we* went to Vegas. Even still, I felt so bad that he was served on Valentine's Day that I asked a friend to bring him flowers thanking him for all the good memories. He texted me to say thank you and that he didn't deserve the flowers. I responded with, "I know…but I wanted you to know I *am* thankful for the good times." He texted me 30 minutes later, "Now I know why you *really* sent the flowers—I just got served."

In the divorce, I stated that I would assume responsibilities for all the debt, but I wanted my Rav4 back. This would leave him debt free (which I thought was generous because most of the debt was spent on him between the attorney to get him out and supporting him over the past five years). He lived with his co-worker so he should have no problem getting to work only a few miles from where they lived. He had my laptop, my nice camera, tons of clothes I bought him when he came home, and I spent hundreds of dollars shipping him ALL his personal stuff, all of which I had bought for him in the first place. You are probably seeing now why he wrote 'once you give somebody something, it's not yours anymore." Cuz I *gave* him a LOT!

Considering he was out of prison seven years early, had a job that I practically got for him, and had more than any other recently released inmate that we knew of,

I thought he should be more than happy to not have any debt.

I actually wasn't terribly surprised when he contested the divorce. I must have been out of my mind, however, to think for a moment that he was contesting it because he thought we could work it out. I seriously thought (and apparently hoped) that filing for divorce might be a wakeup call for him. Nope, he contested the division of property. He thought that *he* should have the car that was paid off (before he even came home from prison) *AND no debt* at all, as it would be a "hardship" for him to have any of the financial responsibility of the debt incurred to make his last several years in prison more comfortable or pay for the attorney who won his freedom. Sometimes I wonder if prison makes your brain not work anymore, or if your brain stop working first, and that's how you wind up in prison. Or maybe your brain work okay while you're in prison, but once you're out, they go all haywire again. Or maybe it was my brain that weren't working; I married a murderer after all. Or maybe—aw, crap, *my* brain are getting all jumbled up now—to hell with it!

He communicated with me via text that he wouldn't *really* leave me with all the debt but that we could work something out, *outside* of the courts. He actually added, "I'm not a jerk, after all. I want to do the 'right' thing by you." Hum…You know that sound a tea kettle makes when the water boils and the steam comes out? Yeah— my ears made that sound when I read that text, as the blood in my brain boiled and steam shot out of my ears. Are you fucking kidding me? I thought. My, Xander— what a great guy you are.

I was more depressed, angry, bitter, resentful, and even suicidal during that time than Vegas is hot in July. During the worst of my depression, I cried buckets and buckets of tears while lying in my bed alone where my husband should have been. I sat on the stairs for hours because I didn't want to sit on the couch alone or want to go up to the bedroom alone. There were *many* days; too many to count, that I would sit in the driveway talking to a friend on the phone for hours, just because I didn't even want to walk in the house alone.

I am *not* afraid to be alone. I was alone all the time during the years before he came home, and I was alone most of my older childhood, but there was something enormously painful about being alone in the house that he picked out for us. Alone in the house that we were supposed to be living in together, as a husband and wife, in the town that was supposed to be our fresh start for falling in love again. Even at my new job, I dreaded leaving work sometimes and often put in 12-14 hour days for weeks at a time before burning out.

I tried to take my life twice; once with a lot of pills (obviously that didn't work since there was a twice), and then again with pills and a lot of alcohol (obviously that didn't work because you're reading this). It was odd that I chose those methods because honestly, I had always thought the best way to go, other than swimming with the killer sharks in Australia, or strapping raw meat to my body and going on a hike in Alaska, would be to lie in the tub and slit my wrists.

I actually thought it through in that I would leave my front door unlocked and leave a note on the bathroom door warning who ever found me to be prepared for a scene of death and that I am sorry for any trauma it may cause them. Even though I had thought this was

the way to go, it seemed so—forgive the expression—
"permanent." I knew there was no way anyone would
find me to save me, whereas with the pills/alcohol
method, it might not work—which I would take as a
sign. I have always been big on signs. I never really
gave much thought to farewell letters though, as I figured everyone would know why I took my life, and
everyone who I *do* love already knows it. I didn't really
give a shit about my stuff, what do I care? I'd be dead;
it's just "stuff."

I took a leap of faith and called my friend Tony
Stubbs (real name because I love him, but also because
he's passed on and hanging out on the soul plane, or
maybe he is back for another round as a sparny tickle,
who knows) who was an author and expert on death
and the soul plane. Anyway, I met him at the nudist
place in Vegas and we would talk for hours about all
kinds of metaphysical stuff. He had some out-there the-
ories, but I loved hearing them and always kept an open
mind to the possibilities that they might be true. I mean,
if we weren't spoon fed stuff like burning bushes, parting seas, and turning water into wine, that stuff would
sound pretty out-there too! Right? I hadn't talked to
Tony in a few years so I was feeling anxious about turning to him during that dark time when he only knew me
when I was happy, and I was pretty sure he would never imagine I could get that low.

I had remembered a conversation with him once
when he told me what happens to your soul when you
take your life. I didn't make a point to retain this information because at the time I didn't think I could ever
conceive of the act. I finally got up the strength to phone
him and with a shaky voice that pretty much gave away

191

why I was asking, I said, "Tony, what happens to your soul when you take your own life?"

He paused, probably to take in the notion of why I was asking, and thinking how best to reply assuming my current state. He calmly yet matter-of-factly replied, "Well, three things happen, 1) You will realize, the moment it is too late, that you fucked up. 2) When you reach the other side, you are shown what your life would have been like had you lived out your soul's purpose; this will suck, and you will realize immediately, that you fucked up. 3) You will be shown how much you hurt those that love you by taking your life. You will see the pain you caused them; this will really suck."

I was speechless. This doesn't happen very often. He then said, "It's just not a good idea. Your soul has a purpose in this life and its purpose is not to end it before it completes its mission this time around." I didn't want to ask him what my soul's mission was; he couldn't really know anyway, and I wasn't sure *I wanted* to know, as I was already overwhelmed with more pressure and pain I could handle at the moment. I was busy wrapping my head around the three things that he said happen when you take your life. I didn't want to hurt anyone, even though there were times I really didn't think anyone cared that much. If they did care, where were they *now* when I needed them the most?

Tony then began to speak louder and more adamantly, telling me that what I needed to do was to help others. I needed to volunteer somewhere to help other suicidal or depressed people. I needed a dog, a lab, to love unconditionally and that would love me unconditionally. I needed to train it to be a service dog to help others. I needed a project bigger than me.

He was getting louder and louder and started a weird hack or cough, I couldn't tell which. He had been a heavy smoker so at first I dismissed it as a smokers cough, but then I sensed something else. I said, "Tony, are you ok? You sound like your crying," he shouted back, "No, I'm not okay, and yes I'm fucking crying. Your spirit guides are nailing me, to nail you, and it's greatly affecting me."

Whoa! I knew Tony had a gift for communicating with the spirit world but I didn't see this coming for some odd reason. Me? *MY* spirit guides were talking to Tony, to help *me*? I was flattered at first, but then confused. "Why are they talking to you and not directly to me?" I asked. He said, "Because they can't reach you when you're spiraling down, you have to reach up yourself, and you are now doing that, through me."

I was never a fan of big dogs so getting a lab was pretty much out of the question, not to mention against my lease agreement. I told Tony I couldn't get a big dog, to which he replied, "Well, get a fucking Chihuahua then." I always loved Tony.

It didn't really surprise me when over the next three weeks or so, labs were popping up everywhere I looked in some form or another. I would smile every time, think of Tony, and thank my spirit guides for the hint/reminder. I went to a local benefit silent auction shortly after our conversation, and at the end of one of the tables, sitting on the floor, was a large print of a beautiful Golden Lab. Because it was on the floor and not on the table with everything else, the dog's eyes were looking right up at me. Our gaze was locked for an eerie moment that felt like forever. I smiled and silently told my higher spirit self, "Ok, ok, ok, I get it.

This is *one* lab I can live with and my landlord will approve of." I bid on it and won it. Ironically, it was my landlord who bought the print from me when I later moved.

Finding a Positive Path

I had an ad on Craigslist for a couple months for a 'roommate wanted'. Only a few people responded—and I ruled out most of them just over the phone; desperate single mothers who were living off welfare and had to move out of their parents' house *immediately* (I can only imagine why if *their parents* were throwing them out). Creepy older guys that asked odd questions about me. People asking if a cat was ok, which pissed me off because my ad said 'NO pets'. The last time I checked, a cat is a still a pet. Note: If you are ever looking for cheap entertainment, place an ad wanting a roommate on Craigslist and then ask them why they are moving out of their current place; trust me, you will hear some crazy shit.

Out of the blue after several weeks of my ad being posted, I got a call from a guy who sounded normal. He was young, had a good job, no pets, and didn't smoke or do dope. He came by and looked at the place and we hit it off. We chatted for almost two hours to get to know each other. He moved in two weeks later.

My new roommate and I were having drinks and deep discussions after dinner one night and I shared my occasional suicidal thoughts with him. Even though we were tipsy, his face turned hard and sober instantly and I swear tears formed in his eyes as he said, "You could do that? Really? You could do that, *to me*?"

My mind also tried to stagger to soberness to catch up to his change in demeanor. I said, in a confused manner, "What do you mean do that, *to you*?" He leaned back a bit and in a way that demanded an immediate and serious answer, said, "Walk me through it. What would you do?" as if daring me to be brave enough to say the words I felt inside, out loud.

I began to tell him my normal thoughts of making the bathtub my final resting place; he quickly cut me off, "...and what? AND HAVE ME FIND YOU? Do you know what that would do to me? I would wonder if I did something, said something, that I caused it in some way, not to mention I would have to live with seeing you like that for the rest of *my* life! We are more than roommates, we are friends, we like each other, we are close, how could you think of doing that *to me*?"

I was instantly sober. Our eyes were locked, and a small amount of tears were welling up in both of our eyes, as we stared at each other for a moment in complete silence. Neither of us blinked for fear a tear would fall. It was sort of an 'I'm not going to give this conversation the satisfaction of a fallen tear' kind of stare off. It worked. We somehow held our eyes open, staring at each other long enough for them to dry out. In that moment, I heard Tony's voice in my head saying, "There's a taste of the third thing that happens when you take your life, just as I told you!" I never gave taking my life another thought.

***

I had started working at a place that made vitamins and I decided that was a sign—the open door to finding a way, *any* way, to climb out of this internal hell. I used every avenue and outlet I could to "get back" to where I was at one time; a state of confidence, pride, and happiness. I started reading tons of self-help and motivational books and material. I started journaling. I started going to meditation classes, seeing movies, taking drives, talking to friends (about positive subjects), seeing a shrink, seeing an acupuncturist, and I even got back on meds again (which I hated again, and stopped after a month or two). I went to a 10-week class called Life Skills aimed at building confidence and self-esteem. I was also enjoying catering to my roommate by making him lunches almost every day, making dinners most nights, and either watching movies together or having healthy and heartfelt conversations after dinner. He didn't mind at all that my making him lunches and dinners was part of my "therapy."

We also did our fair share of drinking, which I actually believe helped. I recently read a quote: "Drinking alcohol has never solved any problems, but neither has drinking milk." I realize any readers in "recovery" or who are family members of substance abusers will protest, but I do believe that drinking with my roommate, in a controlled environment, *was* helpful in *my* recovery from depression. After a while, we actually did taper off a bit, at least during the week, and started taking walks with our neighbor, which also helped my mind a lot.

I really couldn't isolate a single "method" that pulled me out of the pit I was in—perhaps it was a combination of everything, or the drive on my part to get out no matter what, or maybe it was some of those guiding spirits that Tony had told me about. Maybe it was all of it mixed together perfectly like peanut butter and jelly on Wonder Bread.

I do know that meditation *was* a huge help as it allowed for an avenue towards calming my mind in stillness. After several months of going to meditation class at Zero Point, I did it. I woke at the end of the session knowing I had achieved perfect silence of my mind. It was completely euphoric and I floated for days.

A dear friend that I phoned almost daily and who had never-ending patience with me, was also a huge factor in my healing. I don't know what I would have done without his shoulder. The Life Skills class also taught me a lot, but it was being around other people in pain that offered me the most comfort, as we supported and helped each other. It wasn't so much of a "misery loves company" thing; it just felt good, that through my pain, I could help others in that environment—and their being able to help me also made them feel good.

My roommate was a timely blessing for companionship, and I connected with a girl I worked with at my new job that was a true angel. She was very young but had the wisdom, love, and grace of an old soul. She saw my pain and offered a soft hand, always at the perfect times I needed it.

***

On the day of divorce court, thanks to all my little tools, tricks, crutches, and angels, I actually felt ok. I was sure I was doing the right thing, even though it sucked that it had to come to this. I walked into court with the absolute intention that I was going to get my Rav4 back, and also keep all the debt as my original request stated. Even though it was almost "equal" in debt/asset division, it was far from *fair* as far as I was concerned—but I wanted it over. I stated my case. I tried really hard not to sound like the bitter, resentful, angry, hateful, pissed off, hurt, soon-to-be ex-wife, but it came flying uncontrollably out of every pore of my body in completely unleashed fashion.

The Judge listened intently and had a look on her face like "that was interesting, but it doesn't really matter." She then pretty much confirmed the look by stating, "I need to follow the letter of the law and divide everything 50/50 without regard to fairness." She proceeded to violently peck away at a calculator while glancing at the few debts/assets we had. She came up with a figure of something like $2,000 that I would have to pay Mr. Asshole *after* I took all the debt *and* he got the U-Haul truck that I paid for. I said, "Your honor, I don't care what we do or how we split it, I will even give him the Rav4 and keep all the debt, but I will go to jail before I pay him one single dime after all I have spent and done for him."

She asked me some questions about the Corolla and determined that since I just bought it I was severely "upside down" in it. Apparently the "upside down" part counted as debt so that helped to balance the assets/debts out. Then the judge said I just had to pay him a few hundred dollars instead. I gave her the 'I am not fucking kidding, I will set fire to all the vehicles and do prison time before I give him one cent!' look. She acknowledged my look and said, "Okay, you take all the debt including the amount you are upside down on the Corolla, you get the Rav4 back, and he gets the U-Haul." Then, she added most adamantly, "You go down and get the Rav4 as soon as possible and you *make* him come get the truck. If I find out you spent money to bring him the truck, I will be pissed."

There is no way I could say I was "happy" with the outcome, but I had to feel somewhat satisfied. I took the rest of the day off, treated myself to a pedicure, and bought myself a divorce ring.

Xander got one last screw in with the vehicle exchange. It made no sense economically for each of us to drive one-way and each fly back so we agreed to meet half way and do the exchange. I quickly thought I was negotiating with my brother because the "deal" kept changing and I kept getting more and more of the shit end of the stick. First, he couldn't get his trip request with the Parole Office approved in time (I seriously doubted he ever turned one in). Then he wanted to meet at the Nevada border. This meant a much longer drive for me, much more gas money for me, and there was nowhere for me to stay the night after the 10 hour one-way drive.

He then suggested we meet in Winnemucca so I could get a room there. Uh, that is only two hours from Reno, and again, a lot more gas for me. I finally gave up and said, "I'll just drive the U-Haul all the way to Reno and drive the Rav4 all the way back. This way you will not be inconvenienced at all, and I can stay with friends, but you're splitting the gas cost with me 50/50; it's the least you can do." He agreed (of course).

I arrived earlier than we agreed. This was mostly due to me not trusting he would be there and fearing I would have to run around town hunting him down gobbling up more gas in the U-Haul. He opened the door and our eyes locked in the exact same manner they did the very first time; there was heat. Even after our divorce, even after the feelings of hatred, bitterness, and resentment, horrible words exchanged back and forth; the same energy, the same magic, was still there when our eyes met again; at least it was for me, and I am pretty sure he felt something too by the look in his eyes and the unexpected softness in his voice.

It lasted long enough that it had a calming effect on both of us and we managed to be civil to each other. He said he hadn't had a chance to get the money for gas because I was early and asked to meet for dinner... or breakfast, the next day, he shyly added, "Or both" (in the same breath as he stated all he had was $180 which was about 25% of the gas cost, not half). I agreed because I figured $180 was better than nothing, but mostly it was the damn butterflies flapping their wings like they were on crack in my belly again, damn it. I had *never* had anyone have this effect on me, ever. Damn it!

He asked me to call him later to discuss where/when/etc., we would meet for dinner. I decided to keep the faceplate of the stereo from the truck as insurance. He quickly noticed it was missing and said, "Come on, Teresa, I'm not playing games with you, don't play games with me." He looked and sounded so sincere even though he was the master at playing head games. I gave him the faceplate and drove off trusting that he would keep his word. Yes, I realize trying to keep the faceplate was a juvenile act on my part, but it was all I could think of to do to protect myself.

I called him later to confirm our plans as he had asked me to. No answer. I texted him, "Are we still on for dinner?" He finally responded via text, "Have a safe trip home." Wir-Wir-Wir-Wir-Wir – Game Over! I just got played big time and at that very moment I seriously considered rushing to the nearest tattoo shop to have SUCKER inked on my forehead.

I Am... Back

We were officially divorced in June. In early July I traded the Rav4 and the Corolla in for a brand new Rav4 (that was pretty much identical to the one I had that was paid off, minus the smoke smell and ex-husband cooties), and got a check from the dealership for $10,000 to pay off most of our credit card debt that I got to keep. In late July, I was awarded Employee of the Month—and then in August I was fired.

Even though I had never been fired in my life, and the reasons were almost laughable as they were things taken out of context, extreme exaggerations, and outright lies by jealous, small town, small-minded, backstabbing, mindless hicks, I was oddly okay with it.

I have always gotten a little bout of happiness when things end: jobs, relationships, etc. I don't know why, I guess because it relieves the suspense about *will it ever really end?* Yes! It will, and it has. When things end, I now truly do believe that I have the opportunity to start something new. That's great with jobs because there are always other jobs, but the bout of happiness wears off quick with relationships. By the first shitty date when I realized *again* that I hated dating and being single, I *almost* started to forget what was so horrible about my ex. Yeah, I know, hard to imagine, huh? However, have you *been* on a date lately?

At the job from which I'd just been fired, I'd been making shit money when I knew I was capable of earning so much more—so no big loss there. But I loved North Idaho. I knew no matter where I ended up I would earn more money, but I was still pissed I had to leave this beautiful part of the country—this town I loved so much and that helped support me on my healing path.

I often tell people, "Being 'successful' living in Las Vegas is having the means to leave the city to go somewhere beautiful. Being 'successful' living in the Northwest is having the means to have a window to look out of because everything there *is* beautiful."

I used the rest of my month's benefits solely for the EAP program to see my shrink every day; yes, every day. I think it's pretty common to see a therapist once a week or two, so I thought we would drive *each other* crazy if we saw each other every day. To our mutual amazement, our appointments were quite productive. I felt better, more alive, and freer than I had in years.

Even though my counselor and I enjoyed meeting every day, the message he was trying to get through my head, and the conclusion I was coming to, were not quite aligning, so we somewhat playfully butted heads about not seeing eye-to-eye. He tried to convince me that I needed to tame my gypsy ways and get some stability in my life; first get a stable job, then get out of debt, then get in a stable and healthy relationship. I agreed these things *sounded* wonderful, but I sarcastically responded with, "I'll pick some stability up the next time I go to the store; maybe I will find some *stability* in aisle nine."

I *tried* to inform him, that I was not in total control of obtaining a job in this economy and certainly not in that small town. I would try of course, but the decision rested in the hiring company. I therefore had no control over paying my debts off without a job. Finally, even though he suggested I not date (or even flirt with, or kiss a man) for a year, unless I found some dribbling mindless idiot, it was not entirely *my* decision to be in a "relationship" either. Relationships *usually* take another person's efforts and wishes. We went round and round—and it took great love and care on both our parts at times, to not actually get up and wring each other's necks.

Yet somehow, we both managed to call our sessions productive. Love ya, Doc!

I knew I had to find my way back; back to a place where I was last happy—really happy. It was a tool I had learned in Life Skills class: "Do Over!" In other words, try to find a "re-set" place in your previous path that you can go back to, and try another fork in the road. I also did agree with my shrink, though I would never admit it, that I *had* to do this alone. I took a drive around the lake to a little town called Hope. I always think best when I'm driving. I gave some serious thought to finding a place in my past that I was happy, really happy, and happy being alone.

I was actually a bit taken aback and extremely surprised when Vegas popped in my head. I had escaped the city twice; even though I have friends and family there, I hated it both times. Yet, I quickly remembered the time when I became a full-fledged nudist. I had nudist friends there that I went camping, hiking, and walking with. I also had Burning Man friends that I did fun stuff with. I enjoyed feeling part of these free-spirited and supportive communities. I had so many long-term friends there that were smart, supportive, had great jobs, careers or businesses. I knew I would most likely want to leave Vegas again (there is just no curbing this gypsy at heart), but I knew, without a doubt, I had to go back. I could feel it in my soul that this is what I needed to do to re-set my happy clock; to move forward again.

***

I sold just about everything I owned, actually shipped Xander some more stuff, and gave tons of stuff away just before I left. I got rid of every piece of furniture bigger than a breadbox and decided to ship all I had left to Vegas via Fed Ex Ground. That was a mistake by the way; it cost about $200 more to ship my boxes than it would have been to rent a truck and trailer (and keep more stuff). Lessons are learned every day, I tell ya!

I listened to some old Tony Robbins cassette tapes the whole drive down (don't make fun of me, the media might be old, but the content is still good!). I was super pumped when I pulled into town. I had big plans and I was now on the road to success. Unstoppable, I tell ya!

Then my brain gave birth to a baby fear monster.

I sidelined my ambitions of writing this book, working on some ideas and inventions, and even my path to emotional healing, and did the dumbest thing ever. I started dating again. There is nothing like a bunch of attention from men to distract you from achieving true success. I went on 3-5 dates a week for about a month. There wasn't one person I wanted to see a second time, nor did most of them want to see me again either. I was getting frustrated. This distraction was quickly boring me.

I decided to move into a studio with no Internet access. I would then be *forced* to work on my book without the distraction of Facebook, constantly checking my e-mail for jokes from people I haven't actually talked to in 10 years, and the temptation to do online dating again. I would go to my friend's house during the day to use free Internet to look for jobs and come back to the studio to work on my book at night. This was a good plan.

It's always good to have a plan. I was actually thrilled when it half-way worked. I did look for jobs during the day, but I just couldn't find the inspiration to start on this book, my ideas, or inventions. I knew I wanted to write this book first, but there was something about re-living the past to write the first part, and then claiming victory and success at the end, that I just wasn't sure I was emotionally strong enough for yet. Not to mention I wasn't convinced I had achieved "victory" just yet. I spent a lot of time reading and listening to self-improvement and motivational type tapes for a couple months.

I was quickly reaching the decision that dating was just a dumb idea. (Shh, don't tell my counselor that he was right.) It was useless, frustrating, and sometimes painful. Did I mention useless, frustrating and painful? About that time, I decided to find out where my brother was. Now *there* is a distraction! After a bit of investigative work, I learned he was in prison, again, for the third time. Big surprise. I wrote him a letter.

My brother is actually a great guy when he is "inside"—that is, being in a controlled environment. He is funny to the point of making you pee yourself. He is ridiculously hilarious, he is healthy because he is clean and spends his time working out, and he is actually a great guy because he motivates others to do good, work out, and get healthy. Our whole family, and all his friends know all too well, when he gets out, he always goes back to his old ways and he is his asshole self again. (Hell, maybe that's what happened to Xander, too!) But for the moment of time that he is locked up, you get the chance to see him through a window of hope.

He got my letter and called me but we got to talk for only a minute. The prison phone system gives you a teaser minute and then cuts you off by sending you to their automated system, which then rapes your credit card in ridiculous fees to talk to your loved ones. I had shelled out enough money for him the first time he was in prison, for my first rodeo-Tom, and for second rodeo-Xander. I was done spending money, not to mention I didn't have a job, and he would just call and ask me for money anyway. A few days after our teaser call, I got a call from another inmate from my brother's facility. I knew it was really him so I accepted the inmate paid call (they can put money on the phone system on their side to call out also).

I heard a man's voice that was not my brother's. This did not surprise me. What *did* surprise me is how comfortable the voice was even though it had a distinct excitement to it. I had not said anything other than hello so I knew he wasn't excited about that. So this guy says, "Hey, uh, I am just calling for your brother; here, here he is, ok?" And he waited for my answer. There was a giddy excitement in his voice. Why? This thought tugged at me for a moment, then I heard my brother's normal, but also giddy, "Hey, I'm locked-up again so I'm clean, healthy, happy, and funny as hell" voice. We talked for the full 30 minutes allowed before being cut off and forced to bend over for more insane phone charges.

A few days later, he called again using that same guy's phone time. My brother's middle name is "wheeler-dealer" so I figured he had a deal cooking. We chatted for a few minutes and then he said, "Hey, this guy is letting me use his phone time; it's expensive you know, and he is a really great guy to let me talk to you; uh, I love you Teresa, ya know? Uh, you wanna say Hi to him—just to thank him or something?" Aha! *I* am the bartering chip! I had to laugh because I know my brother. I said, "Fine, I'll say Hi."

His name was Xander (strike one), he was the same age as my ex-husband, Xander (strike two); he has done the same amount of time as Xander (strike three). The longer he talked and the more he said, I lost count of strikes he had against him to the point it almost became laughable, yet we were still talking, and somehow our voices were smiling.

He began the conversation with the acknowledgment that he had heard from my brother what I just went through over the past year. He adamantly acknowledged that I would probably want nothing to do with another inmate (he was right, which let my guard down enough to continue our conversation at his expense). He then proceeded to tell me *his* story. Not his story about what he did or didn't do to land him in prison, but what he was going through in *his* current relationship.

He had met a woman through a website just as I had met Xander. They were married the same year Xander and I were. They were in love. About a year previously, (the same time me and my ex finally had our last break up), he had asked a friend on the outside to help his wife with something.

He immediately moved in with her and she stopped writing or coming to visit him. She had chosen a dirt bag (in his words) over him just like my ex chose trailer trash over me. For the past year, as it turns out, he and I experienced the same internal hell of "What did I do? Why am I not good enough? What could I have done differently?" Suddenly the walls came down and I was connected with a new friend. Not an inmate, not a convict, but a human, a man, who had a heart that felt pain just like mine. The same pain *many* of us do.

Over the next month, we talked almost every day. He would call me first thing in the morning so that we could share watching the sun rise together—even though we were miles apart. He would call some evenings and we would compare how different the sunsets looked to each other, in beautiful descriptive detail. Sometimes it's the simplest of things that warm our hearts the most. We vented our stories, we offered each other advice, we smiled, we laughed, we cried, and we fell in love. Some say, "The third time is a charm," and some say, "Three strikes and you're out"; I say the same thing that my beer coozy says, "I am experienced enough to recognize the mistakes I'll make again."

In today's shallow world of the pressure to look and act a certain way to be attractive, and the technical world where everyone is petrified in fear to break out of a life of text messages and email to actually meet face to face, it is so refreshing to spend TIME with someone. Real time, to actually *want* to get to know someone, to try to overcome challenges to *make* it work, to acknowledge the absurdity of what you're feeling, and feel it anyway, just because it feels good, brings joy to your heart, and a smile to your face.

It has been my experience that most people look for flaws too quickly to rule out a potential mate. Sometimes these flaws are obvious, sometimes they don't appear for a few dates, and sometimes the most fatal flaws don't show up for years. Most of an inmate's flaws are a matter of public record and nearly impossible to hide. The reality of my relationships with Tom, who I affectionately call my first rodeo, and Xander, my ex-husband, ended for the same reasons any other's do regardless of criminal record.

Tom had an addiction problem to drugs and alcohol, just like my first husband had to gambling, and just like I had to food. Xander played mental mind games so he could be with other women, which had little or nothing to do with his criminal charges.

In the end, we are men and we are women. We are all human. We all have a choice to seek love or seek hate in one another's human heart. It's really that simple.

The End? Or a chance for a New Beginning?
The only thing that really lasts,
is the memory of the past. –Teresa X. Roberts

AddenDUM
(Assholes Come in All Shapes, Sizes, Ages, and Packages)

Even though you may have been surprised I fell for another guy in prison, it was still a nice ending, wasn't it? At the time, that ending was written I actually *was* in a relationship with another inmate. We really *did* help each other out of our slumps, and for that, I am forever grateful. However, it wasn't long before I recognized that he was a total selfish, self-centered, sex-crazed jerk, and ended it; thankfully, *before* he got out.

I felt this addendum was important to share with you, the reader, how hard I really did try to find a "good guy" and how at the time of this writing, I have found little hope one exists; that is single anyway.

I moved from Vegas to a small town for a big job. While in Vegas, I must have went on 50 dates; I am *not* exaggerating. There was only one guy I saw more than once, and I can't even share (in case there are younger readers and might put this book in a different genre) why he was a jerk, but trust me, he was. When I first moved to this new little town, I went on about 20 dates the first month I was there. Only a couple wanted to see me a second time, but I didn't really want to see *any* of them again.

There was one guy I was slightly interested in, Yuri, but he made it quite clear that he was only there for six months so I was not to "get too attached," so he said. This told me that he was either married or just wanted to have "fun" and nothing serious. Sadly, I sorta liked him. We saw each other a few times, but since we weren't on the same page, it just didn't work.

I put an ad online looking for a room to rent and I got an e-mail from Zack. In part it said, "I live alone, have a big house and I'm gone a lot. I'm 65 and harmless." I was actually a little nervous as to why he felt he needed to say he was harmless, but I figured he 65 so I could probably out run him if I had to. I went to look at the place and I loved it. He seemed pretty cool too. He offered me a beer and after 10 minutes of me jabbering away, and him rhythmically nodding his head, he said, "You talk a lot, don't you?"

He worked in a town two hours away Monday through Thursday so he was home every Thursday night through the weekend and left early on Monday mornings. I had only lived there 10 days when I lost my job. I had some money saved so I wasn't too worried though. I had dinner ready every Thursday night when he came home, and if the weather was nice, we ate on the deck overlooking the mountains. The sunsets were amazing and brilliant in color, and our conversations were beautiful and caring.

Since I had the time, I started a pretty large-scale landscaping project at his place that involved 15 tons of rock. I also did a few things to put a *woman's touch* around the house. After about a month, he started flirting with me a bit. (Did I mention he was 20 years older than me?) Despite the age difference, I was actually growing quite fond of him too. One night on the deck, after perhaps a few too many cocktails, we let our hair down. Well, *I* let *mine* down. He was nearly bald so he let his pants down instead. We started on the deck and finished in his room. We slept together every night he was home for the next several months.

He had a huge and beautiful home. He had not one, but two luxury vehicles, a few toys and some notable assets. The first few months he brought home flowers, left me sweet cards and notes, and said the kindest things. I always had little surprises for him when he came home on Thursdays, and not one Monday morning did he ever leave without a little gift or a sweet note in his car, briefcase, or luggage from me. I couldn't believe it, but I was falling head over heels in love with this old fart.

It had been two long years since my divorce and it was so nice to feel this kind of love, closeness, caring, and affection with someone again. He had been married three times prior, but at his age that didn't really alarm me, as I was at two failed marriages myself. Sometimes he would lean toward me, take my hand in is and hold it ever so tightly and say, "Don't you ever cheat on me; all my ex's left me for other men and I can't go through that again. And don't you ever lie to me; I've been hurt too much to bear anymore lies." As I had also been hurt this way, the minute we became intimate, I stopped dating and was completely dedicated to him.

Despite our active sex life at night, he started to grow distant during the days. A few months into our relationship, he went on a weekend business trip and came home with a framed 5x7 photo of another woman in his luggage. WHAT? He had sex with me all night before he left, and comes home with a framed picture of another woman in his luggage. Who does that? Where does he think he is going to put this thing? Oh, at the place he stays during the week so I would never see it? Wait… what kind of woman gives a man a framed picture of herself? Does she not know he *lives* with a woman already; one that he is currently sleeping with? What kind of possessive freak woman gives a man a picture of herself so she can stake a claim on some nightstand or something in his home. A home she obviously hasn't visited in the last six months. But wait... What the hell… who am I? Do I even exist? Do I even matter? My head was spinning.

I started putting some things together and called him on his lies. For some crazy reason, I honestly thought he would feel bad that he broke my heart, had lied to me, and hurt me so, and profusely apologize, making everything ok somehow. Instead, he asked me to move out, as soon as possible, via e-mail (I would later learn that he had invited *her* to spend the following weekend with him at his house). I had just finished reading his e-mail just moments before my phone rang offering me a job in this shit hole small town. As much as I wanted to pack my things and get out of town that night, I accepted the position through tear filled eyes.

It took me two long years of emotional pain and hell to come to grips with being cast aside for some white trash bitches from my murderer ex-husband who I worked my ass off to get out of prison. Now, I was being cast aside, again, by a man who was 20 years older than me, who was also fat, bald, and had a bum knee, for a woman who didn't even know I lived there? Even though we were only in a relationship a short time, I loved him, in some ways even more than I ever loved Xander. I was devastated.

I had been "let go" from jobs twice in a row and cast aside by men twice in a row. I was a wreck. However, I was very fortunate that I had the tools to heal and knew what to do.

I started drinking heavily again.

Just kidding. I started making lunch dates with my girlfriend, meditating more often, and did everything I could to stay busy.

In conclusion, I truly believe that everything that happens and everyone who comes into your life is a lesson. I was fortunate to love a man who looked like a "great guy" on paper and was sweet as pie in the beginning, yet even though he didn't have a prison record, he ended up being a convicted jerk in my mind (probably his three ex-wives minds too). However, I still think of him fondly and miss him at times, as I do all my ex's.

I truly believe since life seems to keep handing me lemons, it must mean that the universe simply has bigger plans for me; therefore, I shall make lemonade. Only I don't like lemonade, so how about we say I make ice tea instead... while I'm on a long island perhaps.

The Psycho Sequel
(aka Jailbird Jason)
(A word about my brother and
How he leaves you in stitches—
both kinds)

My brother is an abusive asshole who is an oddly creative thief and who is often addicted to drugs. My other sisters and I have scars on our bodies as reminders of what a dick he can be, and my Dad once had to go to work with bruises on his face from my brother beating him up when he was only 15 years old. Sadly, my brother hasn't always been the best father to his five beautiful kids either, to say the least. I cannot stress enough, my brother is an asshole.

However, and this is in no way, shape, or form, meant to excuse the actions that result from the asshole side of him, but he is also the funniest person you would ever meet. He has an incredible charm about him that is 100% undeniable. No matter how much you want to hate this guy, you just can't. He has beat me, stole from me, lied to me, and spit on me, and I still help him when I can. Not because I'm stupid and not because I'm an 'enabler'.... But because I believe, like so many others in his life that he has abused, who also still continue to support him, that he also has some great qualities.

People are never just 'one thing'.

No one is a total saint and no one is a total sinner.

Shortly after my divorce I was, understandably so, going through a depressing time. My brother wrote me the following letter from prison, to try to cheer me up:

Teresa,

If you ever want to feel better about yourself, just strip down naked except for boxer shorts (I know you can do this since you're a nudist). Then duct tape a couch cushion to your chest and put a football helmet on, with the mouth guard in. Then with a tennis racket in one hand and a rusty frying pan in the other, go find the neighborhood retard and chase him down the street. Make sure you limp a little though so he can get away. He will feel good about himself because he got away, and you will feel good because you let him.

The nice thing about this is, when the cops come, they won't know which one of you is really the neighborhood retard, so you can probably get away too. Trust me, you don't want to come to prison, the food is terrible.

-Your little big brother

I sent a draft copy of my memoir 'Why I Married a Murderer" to him asking if he thought it needed anything else. I received the following letter in response:

Teresa,
To be truthful, you need to have the killer chase you around the country trying to find you, and kill you. He finds someone who looks like you in a truck stop greasy spoon and takes everyone hostage until you agree to leave with him. He kills a few fat truckers to show you he's serious, (they were going to have heart attacks soon anyway). The woman who looks like

218

you gets away somehow in a bread box with feet holes cut in it, while the killer is tying up a guy in a wheelchair. Your look-alike in the bread box then climbs in the back of a cattle truck. As she is trying to wiggle out of the bread box, the swat team shoots her to death because they thought she was the killer trying to get away. Meanwhile the killer rolls away in the bread truck and no one noticed because of all the cow casualty carnage. Looks like burgers will be on special for a while.

> *Hope that helps,*
> *-Your Brother*

P.S. I just made parole, can you send money so I don't have to come live with you when I get out?

And this is why…. Most people hate to love him, or love to hate him, depending on whether he's leaving you with stitches from the doctor or stitches from ripping your guts laughing. This is also why I plan to make my brother the subject of my psycho sequel.

Stay tuned.

FREE BONUS CHAPTER

Thank you from the bottom of my heart for purchasing my memoir, and reading it of course. I very much hope you enjoyed a glimpse of the path my life has walked thus far. As a gift to you for purchasing this book (or borrowing/ stealing it from a friend), I invite you to go to www.teresaxroberts.com to read, print, or download a bonus chapter.

Fair warning, you will need this book in hand to obtain the super-secret pass code hidden deep down in the jungles of characters contained in this book. I'm just teasing; I won't make it that hard, but really, you do need this book, so grab a beer and carry it to your web accessible device.

DO YOU HAVE A STORY TO SHARE?

I am looking for unique, interesting, or completely average stories from the pen.

Do you have a significant other inside? Are you inside and have someone you're waiting to come home to? Are you a parent with a child in prison? Are you a parent in prison and have children that someone else is caring for? Are you a Police Officer/Guard/Staff Member and struggle with work vs. home life?

I would love to hear your story. Please send your story only if you approve its use in publication. Please use real names (though I will change them if I share your story). If I do use your story for publication, I may edit it for grammar, but will do my best to not change the overall meaning/content. Please contact me through the website: www.teresaxroberts.com or via the address on the previous page.

***

LOVE THE CHAPTER HEADING ART?
See more artwork from Charles L. Stephenson including the Con-Trolls at: www.chuckstown.com

***

For other writing projects from me, see:
www.teresaxroberts.com

Thank you for reading and I hope you always let love win; Even if you have to fight *with yourself* to get it!

On the Lighter Side

"Reasons why inmates make great lovers"

1. You know where they are every night (and day).
2. They are a captive audience.
3. They are used to being strip-searched and having their privacy violated (however, they are also trained experts at hiding things because of this).
4. They have time to write love letters.
5. They listen and hang on your every word (they may need a bit of information to use against you later after all).
6. When you go to visit, they are so happy to see you (kinda like dogs at the pound).
7. They can't text you pictures of their junk (or text anyone else their junk at 2am from the bathroom in the dark while you're sleeping).
8. You don't have to establish any rules for the boundaries of your relationship; they are already established by the prison system (but you can work *together* to find creative ways to stretch every rule!).
9. They can't take anything from you, which you do not freely give.
10. What woman wouldn't want a man in a cage who is used to adhering to strict rules?
11. When they come home, they will never complain about your cooking no matter how bad it is; they've had worse!
12. When the zombies come, only inmates know how to make weapons out of anything, including toilet paper.

The Author

Teresa X. Roberts has gone from climbing trees in Minnesota, to worshiping the sun in Nevada, to running through the rain in the Great Northwest, where she currently resides... for the moment.

Though she often changes her mind (and men) like the weather, she is also dedicated and passionate about where she is or who she is with....until it ends, that is.

Made in the USA
Columbia, SC
01 May 2022

59688580R00133